AND I THOUGHT 40 WAS OLD

Eighty Years of Tryht!

By

Allyene Palmer

ISBN: 1-4140-0974-7 (e-book)
ISBN: 1-4140-0975-5 (Paperback)

Library of Congress Control Number: 2003097602

This book is printed on acid free paper.

Printed in the United States of America
Bloomington, IN

1stBooks - rev. 10/28/03

This book is dedicated to the memory of my mother, Elsie Edna White and my father, Roy Carl Chrisman; my four brothers, Roy (Toad) and Bob, Howard and Richard, all of whom have gone on before me. Also to my sister, Dora Elizabeth, who still insists she wanted to be like me. And most of all, to my beloved husband, encourager and critic, Richard, and the family we put together — children, grandchildren and great-grandchildren, and their spouses, too, every one loved and loving.

My thanks to my daughter, Carol Hatcher, who read this work and made suggestions that helped, and to Betty McMahon, who patiently proofread the final manuscript.

Cover photograph by Betty McMahon.

Prologue

A strange phenomenon began to develop in the eightieth year of my life. Events of the past flash into memory something like the images on the television screen. They appear in no particular sequence. They come into focus for a time, and then they disappear back into some hidden place. And yet, while they are there, they bring back the very substance of which they were made; sight and sound and scent and feeling. Eighty years! I have inhabited various places on this planet for more than eighty years. When I was sixteen I said that I did not plan to get old. I thought forty **was** old. When I was sixty, I saw my mother's face in my mirror. Now a little beyond eighty, I think it is time for me to sort through the decades of memories to see where I have been and where I am going. And perhaps why I was here in the first place.

In one of my earlier memories, my mother was sitting on a chair in the kitchen reading a magazine. The oven door was open and a pan with the remnants of a roast sat on the oven door. I had been playing with my doll. Why I put the doll into the roasting pan escapes me, but I remember the little naughty thrill of satisfaction I felt. And then Mama rescued the doll, and I learned that I was a bad girl. Maybe it all had to do with my first little brother having invaded my world.

One vivid memory is of being cold. My nose was running. I can still see my fat little hand sticking out of the sleeve of a little puffy wool coat. I was hungry. Then my Daddy came up the sidewalk carrying a white paper bag. I was sitting by myself on a front step, because they needed me to be out of the way while they set up the stove and brought in furniture. We were moving into a different house. Daddy reached into the bag and brought out a sandwich. It was warm. White bread was folded around warm roast pork and a slice of dill pickle. We moved into that house when I was barely four years old. I already had two infant brothers who somehow existed on the periphery of my experience.

Sometimes before I fell asleep, when everything was quiet in our house, I could close my eyes and see wonderful designs. Sometimes, too, I heard what I believed were angel voices singing. These strange experiences of the senses I have never been able to explain, but I can still remember what they were like. I suppose they might be explained as some problems with my eyes and ears. But I prefer to think they were real; perhaps a glimpse into a deeper reality than we can comprehend.

There was a vacant lot next door to that house. There was a stack of boards in the weeds in that lot, and I was standing on top of the pile, loving the feel of the warm wind blowing through my clothes and my hair. I felt there was a presence there with me, having the same feeling of enjoyment with me, and somehow expressing a warm regard for me. I felt loved and valued — I sensed a surrounding affection and approval. I knew Someone was there, though no one was visible. I had no name to call the presence by, but I felt that I knew him.

Table of Contents

Chapter 1

My Mama had all her babies at home. The doctor came to our house. When baby number four was birthed I remember that my two brothers and I were standing in the dark at the foot of our parents' bed, holding on to the white iron rail, and trying to see into the lighted part of the house. Something was going on. Daddy came into the room and said, "All of you get into bed and go to sleep." I think he told us there would be a surprise when we woke up. Much later, I did wake up and Daddy let me come into the kitchen where he and a neighbor woman, Mrs. Helm, were at the table drinking coffee. Daddy told me that I had a new little baby sister. I was not pleased.

Mama did things like bake pies and cookies, and I can remember standing on a chair watching her roll out sugar cookies, my favorite. "Whatcha doing that for?" I asked. "Cat's fur, to make kitten britches!" she told us. When it snowed outside, Mama took us to the window and said, "Look! Mother Carey is picking her chickens." And the swirling snowflakes turned into feathers and down for us.

One time we heard Mama tell Mrs. Helm next door, "If these little nuisances open the door to the Raleigh man again, I'm going to warm their bottoms! That man will talk your head off. You can't get rid of him." Some days later there was a knock at the door, and my brother Toad and I ran to answer it. An enormous man stood there carrying a satchel full of stuff. As Mama came up behind us, the man said, "Good afternoon, Mrs. Chrisman. I just stopped by to see if you need any of our Raleigh products." Toad and I began to cry. "Mama, don't spank us," we begged. "We didn't know it was the Raleigh man! Is he going to talk your head off?"

When Dora was born I was five years old. Childhood in the company of two little brothers, Toad and Bob, and a baby sister who was always on Daddy's lap, was irksome to me. When Howard, baby number five, arrived, he was thought to have been born too prematurely to live. Mama, generally a mild woman, took violent issue with the doctor who wanted to attend to her first. He thought the baby was not going to make it anyway. As it turned out, Howard Lee spent the first days and weeks of his life marinated in olive oil and wrapped in sterile cotton. He lived in an oblong wicker laundry basket lined with blankets and more soft cotton. Mama told us, "His skin isn't finished yet." He was jaundiced and smelly, and his head

2

was way big for his scrawny little body. We were forbidden to get within touching distance of him, not that we would have wanted to.

Mama was cross a lot of the time when Howard was a baby. Dora was still in diapers. And then when Howard was only eighteen months old, Richard Gene was born. He was to be Mama's last baby. Mama hemorrhaged dangerously during that birth, and she told me that while the doctor was tending her, she was floating above the bed. She heard Daddy say, "Oh, God, Elsie! Don't die and leave me with all these kids to raise!" She said she felt irritated and annoyed with him, and wanted to go, but then felt she was being sent back.

As Howard grew, his head was too heavy for his frail body. He did not sit up until he was two years old. One evening, as he tried to maintain his balance, Dora pushed him over, and Daddy laughed. I was indignant and yelled, "That's not fair!" Daddy said, "Go do the dishes." And I stood at the kitchen sink washing dishes while water ran down to my elbows. I was fuming. I elected then and there to be Howard's champion forever. Howard was an awkward little boy, and Daddy had no patience with his lack of motor skills.

Dora was Daddy's favorite, I thought. Actually she was. Always. When she started to school, Daddy said, "Look at Dora. She has only been in school one day, and already she is smarter than Allyene." I did not recognize the joke. He had already told me that I looked like a grasshopper when I crouched on the floor with my knees up around my ears, reading the funny papers. He also had said that my glasses made me look like a hoot owl.

Uncle Ed came to stay with us for a while when he was eighteen or nineteen years old. He was Mama's youngest brother, and I adored him. He had dark curly hair and blue eyes. He laughed a lot, and teased us kids. Once he put an electric wire into a pan of water and threw some nickels and dimes in it. Some of us fished for the change, but I only did that one time. My brothers had more endurance.

Chapter 2

When I started to school I was barely six years old, and small for my age. Then because of class sizes, I was skipped from the first grade to the last half of the second grade. The second grade teacher was Miss Blylie, and I thought she was pretty and nice. I was disappointed to miss her as a teacher when I was moved into Mrs. Iles' room. Mrs. Iles was an elderly woman who looked cross when my classmates and I were brought into her room by Miss Blylie. I blurted out, "I want to be in your room, Miss Blylie. I don't think I am going to like this teacher." And again because of class sizes I would stay in Mrs. Iles' room through that half of the second grade, all of the third grade, and the first half of the fourth grade. And I don't think she liked me!

It was during those years that I came to understand that I was one of the "poor kids." I didn't know that there was a Depression or that our family was poor. This was pointed out to me by one little girl in

5

my grade. She began a song in the schoolyard one morning while we waited for the big door to open. "Allyene Chrisman gets her clothes from the Salvation Army," she sang. Her voice and demeanor were authoritative, and the dozen or so pupils around us began to sing with her. It was a revelation. I had to ask Mama what it meant. It made her cross, and she didn't answer.

Mama fought the Great Depression — and won! It would be hard to describe the battle blow by blow. Of course the highlights had to do with raising six children and a husband in a small, four-room box of a house. I say, "and husband" advisedly. Daddy was a hero in his way, but like a child, he depended on Mama to feed him, coddle him and cater to his whims. Daddy came first. Then came the baby of the particular time, and then we kids, with me as the eldest at the end of the line.

We lined up for a lot of things. Mama fed us cod liver oil in the wintertime. She poured it into a tablespoon, and each of us got a dose, followed by one-sixth of an orange to take the taste out. Oranges were expensive. Mama's cure for a cold was a drop of turpentine on a spoonful of sugar. In the spring she fed us sassafras tea, to thin our blood and make us healthy. And I can remember Mama doctoring us for croupy coughs; rubbing Vicks salve on our chests, and in extreme cases, putting a little on our tongues to swallow.

One day I jumped off the roof of a little shed in our back yard. I landed on a board with a nail sticking up. The nail pierced my foot, stabbing all the way through, between my big and second toes. Mama didn't panic. She stood on the board and pulled me off the nail. Then for days, she poured peroxide through the hole in my foot. It healed.

The Depression didn't really hit us hard until the middle of the nineteen-thirties. Daddy was able to provide for us, and Mama could always stretch a little money and make it go far enough to feed and clothe the first few of us. We could hear her sewing machine going in the mornings after Daddy left for work, and before we first three children were out of bed and pestering for our breakfast which was usually oatmeal with milk and sugar. Mama made my dresses and made shirts and pants for Toad and Bob.

Mama taught us to use our imaginations. Toys, even before the Depression closed in, were few to non-existent. Mama, however, provided us with cardboard boxes, wooden orange crates, and magical items from her cupboards, items we could name anything we wished and they could be whatever we named them.

We acted out the stories from my second grade reading books. We pushed chairs together to make a bridge and played "Three Billygoats Gruff." And we made cupboards from cardboard boxes for

"Boo" to jump out of when we played "The Wee Wee Woman." I was always the director.

Probably the greatest two gifts Mama gave me were the gifts of imagination and of playfulness. Probably the most difficult and demanding thing was the doubtful privilege of being the eldest of six children. When Mama was out of sight, I was responsible for the behavior of the other five of us.

Mama sang to us, too. She had a fair to middling voice, and she knew a lot of songs. She sang "There's a long, long trail a-winding, Into the land of my dreams" and "There's a rainbow 'round my shoulder, And it fits me like a glove." These songs conjured up images in my mind. She sang songs of the First World War and talked about soldiers going away on trains to defend their country, and evoked visions of heroism and longing love.

Mama told us stories, her own stories. She told us about her father, who could invent things and fix things. She told us about Grandpa's garage in Quanah in far away Texas, where Grandpa fixed the early automobiles like the Reo Speedwagon, and where he invented a "perpetual motion machine." We listened and admired. We did not necessarily understand the stories, but we loved the sound of her voice when she spoke of meeting the legendary Indian chief, Quanah Parker, and a woman named Itch-in-the-Nose. Mama grew up in West Texas, and talked about places like Quanah and Childress and Wichita Falls.

Mama, I seem to remember, was generally embarrassed by any show of affection. I can only remember being kissed by her or my father once. I was being lent to an aunt and uncle when I was about nine years old, to baby-sit my three year old cousin Georgie while Aunt Alta and Uncle George picked cherries. Mama kissed me goodbye. I was surprised and uncertain as to how to respond.

Chapter 3

We didn't really understand each other, Mama and I. She told me frequently that I looked like my grandmother Chrisman, a person it seemed Mama did not like. This grandmother was a backwoods Kentuckian by birth, and according to Mama, "still fighting the Civil War." Mama said the old lady had broken a phonograph record that belonged to Mama. It was "Marching through Georgia." Mama also told me that she was constantly nauseated while pregnant with me, because the old lady had insisted that Mama cook her "a mess of black-eyed peas" every day. As a child, I thoroughly believed that I was somehow at fault in this.

I don't remember seeing my Grandma Chrisman ever. She lived in southern Colorado, where I was born. We moved from there to Laramie, Wyoming when I was eighteen months old, and Mama was pregnant with little Roy Junior, "Toad." Then Grandma and Grandpa White came into our lives. Grandpa White said that it was a sin that

Mama cut my hair, that a woman's hair was her crowning glory. What that had to do with me, I couldn't imagine.

Uncle Ed and Daddy were going to remodel the kitchen in the little four room house where we lived. Mama was very pregnant with Richard. Howard was still a baby, and Dora a toddler. Toad and Bob were little boys in rompers. I wasn't quite eight years old. Mama and Daddy had decided that it would be a good thing if Mama took the five of us to Grand Junction on the western slope of Colorado and visit for a month. Daddy could get a pass for all of us on the Union Pacific railroad. Grandpa White would meet us at the station in Grand Junction and take us out to the farm where he and Grandma White lived.

Daddy rode the train with us as far as Denver. We had supper in a restaurant in Denver. It was the first time we children had ever eaten out. Then Daddy put us on the train to Grand Junction and left us. Bob clung to Daddy's leg the length of the car, and then sobbed for a long time after the train started to move. Finally some kind soul gave him a piece of Hershey bar, and Bob gave us all a chocolaty grin. We all curled up on seats in the railroad car and slept. The train stopped at Salida at dawn, and we all got off for breakfast. Cream of Wheat had already been dished out in bowls, sugared liberally and topped off with canned milk. That crust of sugar, and the taste of canned milk, was a breakfast the flavor of which still is satisfying to my taste buds.

I remember the sound of the train whistle in the night. And as the day wore on, I saw wonderful sights along the railroad tracks. There were little huts in fields adjacent to the tracks, and the conductor explained to us that those were for burning charcoal, which would be sold in bags. We crossed the Royal Gorge on a long suspension bridge. We finally arrived in Grand Junction in the early afternoon, and Grandpa was there to pick us up.

Grandpa was a farmer. He had an old truck, too, with which he hauled peaches to town from nearby orchards on Orchard Mesa. Some of us ate too many of those delicious peaches, which became a problem for all of us. We kept the outhouse door swinging, and Mama kept busy washing our underwear.

Grandpa had an old English shepherd called "Old Dick." Old Dick tolerated us, but his only love was Grandpa. That love was returned, too. Whenever Grandpa went to town he brought back a huge peppermint stick for Old Dick, who did not share it with us. Grandpa had asked us kids if we would like a chicken dinner. Of course, the answer was an enthusiastic "Yes!" And Grandpa had brought a bag of candy corn, which he scattered on Grandma's spotless kitchen linoleum. We were thrilled and delighted.

While we were at the farm, Toad fell into an open cistern. He wasn't hurt, but Grandpa had to get a ladder and climb down to get him out. The cistern seemed enormously deep to me, but I suspect it might have been only six feet or so. Just too deep for anyone to be able to reach Toad.

My brothers and I had fun sleeping in and jumping on a feather bed in a huge built-in bunk. It enfolded us in warmth and softness. We looked forward to bedtime, and even accepted naptime in that cozy, welcoming place.

Our Aunt Daisy, who lived with Grandma and Grandpa, had a man friend. His name was Cal. He teased us, and he took me for a ride on one of Grandpa's work horses. It was my first horseback ride, and the very last one I really enjoyed.

One day Cal and Daisy took me with them to a sheep camp, high on a mountain. The only thing I remember about that day is that Cal held me by my heels over the edge of a high cliff, on a road called the "Serpent's Trail." I was terrified beyond being able to cry as I hung there, seeing evergreens that looked inches tall, far below. I can still feel the perfect despair that caused me to have nightmares for years. Nightmares of high places and helplessness.

I missed Uncle Ed. I remembered the comfort of snuggling close to him on the davenport as he read his "Western Story" pulp magazines. I even missed his teasing, which seemed much less cruel than having Cal hold me over that cliff.

Daisy and Cal were eventually married and moved away from Grand Junction to a farm between Fort Collins and Loveland, Colorado, many miles closer to where we lived in Laramie. Some years later, Grandpa White died, and Grandma moved to a farm near Cal and Daisy. I never got to know Grandpa White better, and Grandma White had no doubt seen enough of us during our visit to Grand Junction.

Grandma White, I came to realize, didn't approve of Mama's ways of doing things and she thought my siblings and I were an ornery and crude bunch of little ruffians. We didn't have much of an upbringing, probably because there were six of us between the ages of two and ten by the time Grandma White spent any more time with us. My little sister Dora was the only one of us who charmed that gruff, outspoken ninety-pound critic who was our Grandma White. We saw this grandmother only once in a while. That suited her. And us. My Mama was clean, but she wasn't tidy. She cleaned the insides of cupboards and washed walls and windows, but the ironing never got done. We had only two tiny closets in the little four-room house in which Daddy and Mama were trying to raise six of us without killing any of us or allowing us to kill one another. It was, after all, the Depression.

Grandma White lived for several years with Aunt Daisy and Uncle Cal in Colorado. Once in a great while I got to visit for a week or two. I equated Colorado with its farms and cherry orchards with heaven and I loved to visit there and go to livestock sales with my uncle and go swimming in Buckhorn Reservoir and have picnics that ended with ice cream made in an old hand-crank ice cream freezer. Life in Laramie during those years was uneventful.

Grandma White and Aunt Daisy **ironed pillowcases and dishtowels and sheets!** They also embroidered everything in sight. Mama finally outdid them, though. She eventually crocheted bedspreads for Dora and me, and for the wives of all my brothers. Mama tried for a while to teach me crochet and knitting, but, as she later confessed to a neighbor, "Allyene is all thumbs." I didn't really understand these crocheting and embroidering women, and they didn't really understand me. However, I could always spell crochet even if I couldn't make my fingers do it.

Early one morning, on one of the cherished visits in Colorado, I awoke to find a turkey on my blanket looking into my face, and what looked to be hundreds of turkeys gobbling and staring, all around me. I was sleeping on a cot in an unfinished basement under the new house my uncle was building for his family. Turkeys are probably the dumbest things in the world, just next to sheep. A woman was herding them. She was a raw-boned, talkative woman, and she herded the turkeys the same as sheepherders herd their sheep. That day she showed me a rattlesnake skin longer than I was tall. She had killed that rattler and skinned it to protect her flock and she had collected a lot of snake skins that way. Turkeys eat grasshoppers and that was a big grasshopper year. Maybe it was a big rattlesnake year as well.

Chapter 4

Things got really bad for our family in the depths of the Great Depression. One day we heard our Daddy say, "By God, if things don't get better soon, we might have to eat these kids." In a nightmare I had after hearing this, I dreamed my mother was stuffing Toad into a sausage grinder attached to the kitchen counter. And another time I dreamed Daddy lifted the round stove lid on the kitchen range and trying to put Toad into the fire.

Daddy went to work for the WPA for a short while during one of the coldest Wyoming winters ever. With a group of other men, Daddy rode in the open back of a truck, thirty five miles to and from work. The temperature was in the minus thirties, and one of the men had a bottle of whiskey, which he passed around. Daddy, along with the others, took a healthy swig for the warmth it provided. And my Mama had a fit when she smelled it on his breath. Her aversion to alcoholic beverages was intense. She shared with us that she had an

17

uncle who was addicted to alcohol to the extent that he would drink vanilla or lemon flavoring, or even Sterno, for the alcohol in them.

At the very worst of the Depression, Daddy said to Mama, "Well, Elsie, when you get to rock-bottom, there is no way to go but up." I have thought about that statement many times in the course of my life since then.

During that period of the Depression, in the years while Adolph Hitler was rising in power over in Europe and the economy in the United States was at its lowest point, Mama began to engage in her battle. She sent for government pamphlets instructing mothers on how to raise their families and keep them healthy on little or no money. Mama could stretch a dime's worth of hamburger to make a whole skilletful of water gravy. She seasoned it with plenty of salt and pepper, and made a pan of water biscuits to go with it. She could take a little cubed beef and make a stew of potatoes, carrots, an onion, a turnip and a jar of home-canned tomatoes — she made it taste good with a little seasoning, and we ate it with gusto.

We always had a little garden in the summer. Spring greens from the garden, with a little dandelion and lambs quarter, were washed and "picked over" by Mama. She fried a slice or two of bacon and crumbled them, and then while the skillet was still hot, poured in a little vinegar. This was poured over the greens and they were "wilted." It was with this kind of food that my mother kept us fed and healthy — a little skinny, perhaps, and worrisome to the school nurse, when chubbiness was thought to be a sign of good health and nutrition.

The grocery store was just around the corner from our house. The feel of it still lingers in my mind as a good childhood memory. It was not like the modern supermarket. Cookies were in enormous wide-mouth glass containers — sugar cookies sparkling with coarse sugar sprinkles, molasses cookies with anise frosting up to the edges, big oatmeal cookies loaded with raisins — to be carefully chosen and counted out and carried home in a brown paper bag. The candy counter was at the front of the store. There was a mind-boggling assortment from which to choose, should you happen to have a penny to spend; little chocolate cigars with pink and white marshmallow inside, licorice pipes, penny suckers and jawbreakers — it could take half an hour to spend a penny, and the storekeeper, Mr. Roush, would wait patiently and sympathetically for you to make your selection. He knew how seldom you had a penny or two to spend.

At Mr. Roush's store meat was freshly cut and was wrapped in white butcher paper tied with string from a huge spindle on the wall. Our mail carrier frequently stopped at the store for his noonday lunch — and the children of the neighborhood followed him into the store and watched in fascinated awe as the grocer ground raw beefsteak, mixed it with a raw egg and piled it on a slice of white bread, salted and peppered it generously and topped it off with a generous slice of Bermuda onion. A raw-meat-eating postman brought color and excitement into what was often a pretty stale day.

Chapter 5

During those childhood years with four brothers and a sister, I began what would be a lifetime feud with my father. He didn't like me, and I didn't like him. Our arguments were fierce and, oftener than not, got me yelled at or slapped. Sometimes Mama didn't like me much, either. According to Mama, when she talked with Grandma or my aunts, "Allyene has always been stubborn, ever since she was born." Or, "Allyene will always argue, no matter what you talk about." And then, when I was twelve years old or so, "Allyene can't walk out the front door without stumbling. She is the awkwardest kid in this world." And I was. Stubborn, mouthy, argumentative and awkward. And resentful and sarcastic and impatient. "I named her after a girl who spent her life in a wheelchair. She was so sweet and gentle and patient, and I hoped Allyene would grow up to be like her." I did not. Maybe my parents didn't like me much, but I knew I could depend on them to take care of me, and that was love.

Uncle Ed and Daddy went together to buy a car one time. It was a nineteen-sixteen Maxwell. It had funny wire wheels and skinny tires. We kids watched in fascination one day when a tire came off and rolled ahead of us down the road. We bumped alongside of it on a naked wheel until it fell over and we caught up with it and it could be repaired and put back on the rim. We were on the road from Laramie to Fort Collins, Colorado. It was partly a dirt road, and dusty. The horn said "ah-**oo**-gah! ah-**oo**-gah" as we rounded curves marked "Sound Horn." This car was a roadster, so we all sat in it with the sun beating down and the wind whipping our hair into our eyes. It was great adventure. In Colorado the grass waved on the hillsides like water running down.

Toad, and my next brother, Bob, affected my life during my early teens about like mosquitoes or flies buzzing around, except when Mama and Daddy went to the grocery store or a movie and left me in charge. Everything was expected to be in good order when they came home, and this expectation sometimes made it necessary for me to exercise some big sisterly muscle. There were lots of little boys in our neighborhood, and when Daddy and Mama were out of the house, all of them ran through the four little rooms we lived in, yelling like little Comanches and making a mess. I could whip most of them in a fight, until my brothers started to outgrow me, and I had to begin using diplomacy, like, "Here comes Mama with a switch!" Sometimes it worked.

What I remember most about Toad and Bob were their little male contests. "I can pee higher than you!" they bragged, and proved themselves by making their mark on the sides of the shed in the back yard. They also trailed me around and bored me to death with their shenanigans and idiotic jokes.

And then there was Dora Elizabeth, just between Toad and Bob, and the "little boys," Howard and Richard. Dora was a complete tomboy. Mama always made her little-girl dresses with puffed sleeves and sashes. The sashes were usually torn loose on one side and dragging shortly after Dora was allowed outdoors to chase after the boys. She climbed fences, walked across shaky boards in the loft of a big barn next door to us at Mrs. Warren's house. Dora says now, "I always wanted to be ladylike, like you and your friends." I don't think so.

My friends were Maxine and Darolyn. They were sisters. They lived three blocks down the street from us. They had two younger brothers and a little sister. Maxine was more or less ladylike, and Darolyn was a tomboy. We ran up and down alleys in the early evenings playing hide-and-seek and run-sheep-run. Maxine usually quit early in the game and went home, but Darolyn only quit when she was bleeding from a barb-wire cut or a knee that was too skinned to ignore. My participation was generally of shorter duration than Darolyn's, too. I much preferred to read.

When I was in the third grade, a girl named Janet loaned me her copy of *The Wizard of Oz* and this book initiated for me a life-long love of reading. I read all the Oz books, and then a series of Miss Minerva books, which were by today's thought, totally lacking in political correctness, but altogether charming, with Miss Minerva and her housekeeper, Peruny Perline and Peruny Perline's son, P-Sam. From those, I graduated to the Ann books by L. M. Montgomery. For reading I had a special place behind the pot-bellied coal stove in the living room. I could crouch in that corner reading for hours and nobody would notice unless Mama had a chore for me.

Chapter 6

Actually I had learned to read in the first grade. Daddy had me sound out the words in the newspaper and read articles to him. Will Rogers had a column in the daily paper and Daddy would laugh at his humor. Daddy took me to the library, too, and introduced me to the librarian, Miss Ruby. For years I spent Saturdays at the library. I was allowed to fill up my parents' library cards with my chosen books, if I would pick one out for each of them. Daddy liked Zane Grey, and Mama read Kathleen Norris and others whose names I have forgotten.

When I was in the third grade I came home excited on Lincoln's birthday and began telling Daddy about the freeing of the slaves and other things we had learned that day about that great man. Daddy was furious. "Don't you tell me about that old n— lover, you don't know the least farthing thing about abelincoln and neither does that half-witted teacher!" I was astounded and hurt.

Daddy was prejudiced against everyone in the world except southerners and American Indians. He claimed to have some Cherokee blood. Unfortunately, I was a stubborn and argumentative child, and my father was an impatient, profane and sometimes violently angry man. Our confrontations were frequent.

Both of my parents were brought up in the rural south and both were limited in both education and experience. Then, after they married and began a family, they were trapped into an endless struggle which, as the Depression deepened, seemed ever more hopeless. In nineteen thirty-two when I was ten years old and the Depression seemed to be an endless part of life, the picture of Franklin Delano Roosevelt hung in our living room, a focus for the hopes of my father and others like him whose futures seemed to have no hope. I truly got the notion that Roosevelt was next to God and would rescue us from that miasma of poverty that seemed to threaten to smother our family and many others in our community.

During my childhood years Daddy spoke "hillbilly." He said "haint" and "caint" and used colloquialisms like "least farthing thing" and told me when I got too smart, "You haint nobody's great-grandmammy; haint nobody got to look up to you." I wasn't quite sure what that signified. But when I confided that my teacher had told me that "haint" and "caint" were wrong, I was put in my place.

My father came from Kentucky hill country people, although he himself was born and raised in rural Oklahoma in the late eighteen hundreds and around the turn of the century. His father died when he was only nine years old, and he had to take on the responsibility of the farm. He had only a third grade education. He took care of his mother for years. Shortly after the end of the first world war he moved with her to southern Colorado, where he and my mother met and married.

Daddy told me once that when he was a child on the farm, he had been sent to bring the cows in for milking. It took a while to find them, and when he was bringing them up through the lane it grew very dark. He described how scared he was. He was scared enough to run, but he was also too scared to! I could feel that fear, and identify with that little boy whose knees were jerking with every step.

Daddy was the youngest of fourteen children, and was born late in his mother's life. He had nieces and nephews who were much older than he. He only knew a few of the names of his brothers and sisters. He was born in eighteen ninety-five in rural Oklahoma. As he described it, there was no mail delivery where his family lived. When the brothers and sisters grew up and left home, they were seldom heard of again. Daddy did tell us that two of his brothers rode in on horseback one day, and he thought that they had been riding with a gang of outlaws. He told us, too, that not long after his father died his

27

brother Jim had been accidentally shot climbing through a fence with a rifle in his hand. There were three sisters that he knew, Molly and Minnie and Allie, and a brother Alonzo, nicknamed "Blackie." We heard that Blackie had lost a leg in a coal mine accident down near Pueblo, Colorado sometime in the late nineteen-twenties or early thirties.

My grandmother White and my aunts did not care much for my Dad. And when they visited, Dad didn't hang around the house. He found things to do. Aunt Daisy told me once that my mother had always been jealous of her. And added that my Dad had made a pass at her. To my everlasting shame I shared the first with Mama, bringing tears to her eyes, and thank God I had the good sense never to mention the second.

Daddy bucked ties for a living when I was very young. Tie buckers carried railroad crossties from railroad cars and stacked them in the railroad yard, criss-cross to the height of a man. Dad was only about five feet six or seven inches tall, with muscular shoulders and arms from the hard physical labor. He wore a horsehair pad on his shoulder when he worked, and Mama sometimes had to doctor a boil that formed under the pad.

When I was in my teens, Dad began working nights at the plant where the cross-ties were treated with creosote and steam to preserve them. He worked there as a laborer for some time, but determined to do better than that, he managed to memorize the ratios of creosote to steam pressure to board feet of ties, and to pass the examination to become a timber treater, or "stationary engineer." He always continued to work nights, and was irritable with us kids most of the time.

Chapter 7

Laramie, Wyoming, is as cold a place as you will find, I think, in the whole North American continent. Laramie sits on a high, wind-swept plain in the Rocky Mountains. There is a joke about the Wyoming wind. If it ever stops blowing, all the people in Laramie (or Cheyenne, if that is where you live) will fall flat on their faces. Or, if the chain that is hanging on a pole in the center of town gets to be perfectly horizontal, people know the wind is blowing. Signs in grocery stores try to answer the most-asked tourist questions. One reads, "Yes, the wind does always blow here."

Summer or winter, it was always a challenge, walking in the wind twelve blocks home from the public library with a pile-high stack of books in my arms. And it was good coming into a warm house and having Mama make a cup of hot cocoa and some toast, to take the chill away. Then the coziness of opening the first book and snuggling down behind the heating stove in the living room.

Richard Gene had a perfect rose branded on his skinny little bottom when he was five or six years old. After his bath one evening he ran into the living room clad only in a towel and backed into the chromium, ornately decorated circle that was meant to protect people from getting too close to the pot-bellied stove. The rest of us all thought his rose was cute.

One cold day when I was in junior high I was walking to school in the company of two other girls, when one of them said, "What **is** that?" We all looked down to see. What it was, was a long trail of brown stocking snaking along behind me, dragging in the sooty wet snow on the sidewalk. There was a big hole in the sole of my shoe, and it had been fixed with a piece of cardboard inside the shoe. I hated wearing long stockings when everyone I knew wore what we called "half-sox," so I folded my stockings back and forth under my foot until the part that showed was short enough to please me. The cardboard in my shoe had disintegrated in the wet, dirty snow, and that stocking had escaped and there it was, my guilty secret revealed.

Now and then a chinook hits Wyoming at odd times during the year. A chinook is a soft, balmy wind out of the south that startles and elates Wyomingites when it comes. It melts the ice and snow, and confuses us into thinking that maybe the climate has changed for the better. It generally follows a spell of thirty below zero weather.

The night of the Junior Class Play at Laramie High School in nineteen thirty-eight was made memorable by the fact that the temperature rose to the high seventies, and the air grew soft and damp. It was the middle of December, and was one of the loveliest evenings of my life. The applause of the audience echoed in my ears as I walked toward home after the last curtain went down. I reveled in the softness of the evening air and the glow of the evening just past. The night air held the incomparably pure scent of prairie grass after a rain.

Chapter 8

Miss Bulger was one of my eighth grade teachers. She was a tall, lanky spinster with an exceedingly wrinkled face, hooded eyes and a large nose. She looked like we pupils imagined Ichabod Crane, about whom we were reading, to look, and she was one of the kindest people I ever knew. She encouraged me to enter an essay contest sponsored by the Reader's Digest. I won it. I think I got all of five dollars, which I gave to Daddy and Mama. As I recall, they were pleased and proud, especially when my success was mentioned in the Laramie Republican Boomerang, our one (at the time) newspaper. I was so emboldened by this accomplishment that in my sophomore year in high school I convinced the editor of a short-lived weekly paper that the one thing his paper desperately needed was a column about doings at Laramie High School. I got a by-line and three dollars a week for a short while until the paper folded.

During the summer following my second year in high school I made a terrible mistake. My friend Darolyn and I had been out with a group of friends. I had orders to be in by ten o'clock, and I was. The only thing was, no one else had such a restriction, and when we pulled up in front of my house, everybody said, "Ask if you can't stay out a little longer." I tiptoed in and whispered at the door of Mom and Dad's bedroom, "Mom? Dad?" Not a sound from them, so I tiptoed back out to the car and we spent another hour and a half having fun, and then they took me home. I said my goodnights and let myself quietly in the front gate. When I looked up, there sat Dad and Mom on the front step, waiting for me. It was with a sick, sinking feeling that I heard, "Well, Missy, you won't be going out again **this** summer!" And I didn't. I wasn't allowed to leave our yard, except trailed by four younger brothers and a little sister, or some combination of the same. It was a very long summer.

I was an ungrateful and ungracious teenager, and given to saying cruel things. Once I said to Dad, "People who can't afford to take care of children shouldn't have them." I was immediately ashamed, but I didn't know how to apologize, and the moment passed. I had been in a snit because I thought I needed some new clothes and there was no money for such. I don't think I ever apologized, but I really was sorry.

Once, when I was just out of high school, Daddy said a thing that changed my view of him (for a short while!) and gave me a new view of myself. I had fallen in love for the first time in my life, with a young student at the University. His name was Dick, and he was handsome and charming, and he seemed to like me a lot. He was being sponsored by an aunt who taught mathematics at the University. She was also helping to finance his education. There came a time when she told Dick that he was spending too much time with one girl, and he should be dating around. Obediently he made a date with a girl named Jeannie. He had sung songs to me in a good baritone voice; songs like "Blue moon, you saw me standing alone," and he said my hair reminded him of a dark waterfall. I imagined him singing to her, "I dream of Jeannie with the light brown hair," and the next time I saw him I slapped his face and walked away. Then I moped and cried for weeks.

One day my Dad put his arm over my shoulder and said, "I know you are really hurting, Sis, but I know you are strong. You will come out of this with flying colors one of these days." It was a startling moment and it gave me a new vision of myself and a little different view of my Dad.

Chapter 9

From the time I entered the third grade, I chose to go to the First Baptist Church every Sunday. Janet, the lender of the Oz book, invited me. When I was fourteen I decided to be baptized. Daddy was against it. "Those people are just a bunch of damned hypocrites," he yelled. "All they want is your money." This seemed ironic to me, in that I had never had any money to worry about, and I had no idea what was a hypocrite. All I knew was that the Sunday School teacher and a group of Baptist young people were my friends. Mrs. Nolan was our teacher. She moved up with us each year from the third grade through high school. Daddy said, "I don't know what you see in that old sow," and "If you insist on getting baptized you'd better not backslide or you will go to hell." I thought, "Well, maybe."

There were seven of us girls who formed the nucleus of our group of young Baptist girls, and others came and went. There were Maxine and Eileen and Carol and Janet and Ruth and Mary Ethel. Mrs. Nolan said we were like spring flowers, the summer we were sixteen. We did Sunday evening programs at the church, singing good Baptist hymns and reading out of the Bible. We went on hikes and camping trips, and Mrs. Nolan saw that we were fed and kept warm and dry. Maxine and I got caught in a rainstorm and before we could get to shelter we were soaked and chilled through. Mrs. Nolan fussed and scolded and got us into dry clothes and made sure we didn't catch cold. Hot tea was her solution for most problems. We waded in a mountain stream and got leeches fastened on our legs, and squealed as Mrs. Nolan picked them off.

We went in the summer to Camp Wyoba up on a mountain outside Casper for two weeks. We hiked and ate camp food and boys and girls paired off and surreptitiosly held hands around the campfires in the evenings, shivering in the chill mountain breeze. Innocent romance, more in love with our young selves than with each other. For the rest of the year we waited anxiously for the mailman to bring letters from the friends we made at camp. It was a peaceful time. We gave little thought to the future then.

Daddy didn't believe in churches, but once he told us that in the minutes before his father died, he had opened his eyes and smiled, and said that the angels had come for him. So I guessed that Daddy believed in some kind of hereafter.

Anyway, I was baptized. In a white robe I stood neck deep in a pool behind a curtain and the Baptist minister put his hands on my shoulders and gently pushed me under the water. Three times. In the name of the Father. And the Son. And the Holy Ghost. I expected to feel different but it was still just me with wet hair stringing down my back. After the service was over and people had gone I sat on the church steps. All I felt was lonesome. It seemed like there should have been some kind of celebration. So I went home. No one said anything and I didn't say anything either. All the same, I was a bona fide Baptist. Mrs. Nolan and my Baptist girl friends surrounded my high school days. Daddy got used to it. And I don't think I ever was a backslider. At least not for years and years. I believe I would have heard about it if I had been.

There was a story in Mama's family that when Grandpa White was a little boy, he went and stood at the foot of his parent's bed one night in the middle of the night and said, "Pearlie is gone. You'd better come." When they went to his sister Pearl's room, they found that she had died in her sleep. Little Robby, my grandfather, slept in another room and they were puzzled and asked him how he knew she had died. "Pearlie came and told me she was going," he said. This story was recounted whenever Mama and any of her family got together. And sometimes when it was just Daddy and us, Mama shared it again.

My understanding of life was that there was a God up in heaven, but the way I thought about him was colored somewhat with my relationship with my Dad. Also, I had been told in Sunday School that our lives were like personal notebooks kept by God, and that any blots or stains would be judged when we died. Since I was always getting blots and stains, I pretty much believed that I was a hopeless case. Though I avoided doing the really bad sins, like stealing and lying, except in unusual circumstances. Sometimes I could live with a little guilt.

One beautiful summer evening, just at dusk, all the neighborhood kids were playing hide-and-seek. I joined them, and I was hiding under an enormous lilac bush in our yard. No one had found me for a long time. I was just sitting there enjoying the scent of the lilacs and the beauty of the evening. The first stars were just beginning to come out, and there was a crescent moon. Suddenly I was filled with a feeling of joy; of being at one with everything. Someone whose presence I could feel was there with me, liking what I liked and liking me.

Chapter 10

Nineteen thirty-nine was the year of my graduation from high school. Franklin Delano Roosevelt had been President for seven years. Daddy had worked his way up to stationary engineer or timber treater, and was making the best money of his life. William L. Shirer was broadcasting from Berlin where Adolph Hitler and the Nazis were on the move, and the news seemed threatening. I was on the high school debate team and our topic for the year was "Resolved: that the United States should establish an alliance with Great Britain." Our team could debate either side of the question and win.

That year a young German student named Werner visited our school. When he was asked about the Nazi party, he stiffly informed us that he was not permitted to discuss politics or his homeland. At odd moments during my life I have wondered how he fared through the years, and whether he survived the war in Europe.

It had been pretty much established that I would not be starting to college in the fall. "You know we can't afford it, Sis," Dad said. "You'd better be thinking about getting a job." Dad had firm opinions. "You don't need to go to college," he told me. "You're a girl, and you'll have a husband to support you some day." He had already informed me, "You don't need to learn to drive. You have four brothers and me. We can take you anywhere you need to go."

It was true then that a college education did not suffice to guarantee a job. College graduates were having to settle for jobs driving taxis and waiting tables. World War II had not yet occurred; it had not yet brought about the great middle class that would be created by all the wartime jobs. We hadn't yet met Rosie the Riveter. The summer of thirty-nine was becoming pretty boring.

Then I met Dick from Nebraska, that singer of love songs. Soon after, a handsome man somewhat older, appeared at our door one evening. He said that he had heard that I was talented and that I enjoyed acting. He was Steve Cochran, who with his wife Florence Lockwood, was getting a cast together to stage a performance of *East Lynne* in a structure at the western edge of town known as the Bloody Bucket, formerly a bar. He invited me to play the role of Barbara Hare. I was enchanted. The experience was fun. After a month of rehearsals performances ran nightly for two weeks. Audiences were appreciative. Dick brought me roses. Florence looked at me

41

curiously as I held the flowers. There were only three professionals in the entire cast: Florence, who was a real beauty with a Liz Taylor kind of glamor and gorgeous purple eyes; Steve, her husband, who was dark and handsome, and another less glamorous figure named Bob who directed.

That was an enchanted autumn, but all good things must come to an end. All bad things, too, of course, but that seems to take a lot longer. The Playbarn Theater, as the Bloody Bucket had been renamed, was closing. Steve, Florence and Bob were heading for California to try for movie careers. Daddy had taken to referring to Steve as "that lounge lizard," and I knew that he was about to put his foot down. I had been staying out all hours, since the cast went to a Chinese restaurant for food after the performances. And I had been sleeping until noon, which Daddy, who worked nights, felt to be a privilege that had to be earned. Steve and company wanted me to go with them to Hollywood, but the idea was too scary. Years later I saw Steve Cochran in a few B-grade movies.

Soon after Steve and company left Laramie, I enrolled at the University; having recovered from the heartbreak of my first love, perhaps not with "flying colors," but well enough to pull myself together. I was midway into the first semester. One day I came home from my classes and Dad said, "I found you a good job, Sis." I didn't argue.

Dropping out of college was not as painful as I would have thought. My courses were fairly easy, and I had spent a lot of time in the Student Union, trying to learn to play bridge and getting acquainted with some male students.

One young man made a deep and lasting impression. His name was Michel Korjelski, and I liked him a lot. He walked me partway home from time to time. He was funny; full of jokes and laughter. He had bright, sparkling eyes, and I enjoyed his company.

One day, Michel grew very serious. He was a Polish Jew who had been born in China, where his parents still lived. He told me that he was learning to fly airplanes so that he could go back to China and fight in a war in which he was certain the United States would eventually have to participate. Years later I wrote a poem, "Afterthought, 1962," about this conversation; I ended the poem by describing my own inability to hear his words; which "sliding down the bright, impenetrable mirror of incomprehension, slipped to the sidewalk and lay between us for these more than twenty years," words not understood, until my life and the lives of everyone I knew became tangled into the war he saw coming.

Someone in a creative writing course I took later said that Michel was a "cliche." Perhaps so, but while I knew him, and later when I

43

heard that he had died in that war, he was more than a cliche; he was one of the many heroes whose names and faces had been familiar and dear to me. Not so easy to dismiss, for me.

With Dad's blessing, I went to work as assistant to the bookkeeper at a lumber and construction company. I worked there for a year. I wasn't very good at it. And it seemed like a very boring year. The one bright thing was that I earned seventeen dollars and fifty cents every two weeks. Dad took ten dollars of it, and I got to spend all the rest on myself, and besides, I graduated from oatmeal to coffee and sweet rolls for breakfast. Having reached adulthood had its rewards.

Chapter 11

One night in late September, Darolyn and I went to a "mixer" at the University. I proudly wore a short, Kelly green skirt and a brightly embroidered yellow sweater, my parents' gift for my eighteenth birthday the week before. Pete, who was a student in his second year there, told a friend when he saw me that he was looking at the girl he was going to marry. We danced to "In the Mood" and dated for about four months. Pete had cute eyebrows and a cocky attitude, and he was a great dancer. We did most of our courting in the rumble seat of a friend's Model A, which had been christened "The Flying Coffin." It could go eighty miles an hour coasting out of gear down the hill from "the Summit," which was the highest point on the highway across the United States. An enormous bust of Abraham Lincoln marks the summit now.

We told Dad that we wanted to get married. I don't remember what Dad replied, but he later told me he thought Pete was a "good guy." Forgiveness must have been somehow figured into our family relationships. Mom and Dad never completely wrote me off, no matter what. Mama sat beside my bed for a while the night before I was leaving to be married. She didn't tell me anything; she was much too shy to do that. And Dad gave me a sort of quick and careless hug the morning I left, and said, "Take care of yourself, Sis." I was dressed in a purplish wool dress with a hood, trimmed in black velveteen. I wore high heels. At the last minute I noticed that there was a run in one of my stockings, but I couldn't do anything about it.

Since there were still five kids left to raise, I am sure that both Mom and Dad were happy to see me off. In fact, they sold the house in Laramie and moved to LaPorte, Colorado, shortly after I left. They bought a little farm there. For six months I didn't know they had moved. Mom was a great talker, but she wasn't much of a letter writer.

The next twenty years of my life began that day with a trip to Rawlins, Woming, which was at that time a little ethnic whistle-stop on the route of the Union Pacific Railroad. A two-lane highway, US 30, ran through Rawlins, after passing through Medicine Bow and Hanna.

When we reached Rawlins we went to the justice of the peace and got a marriage license. It was lunch time, so we had to wait while the justice of the peace went to lunch. His secretary would be one witness; Pete's cousin Everett would be the other. While we waited we went to eat at a little cafe where someone was so enamoured of the song, "San Antonio Rose" on the jukebox that it played over and over while Pete and Everett ate and I nervously played with my food (a country-fried steak with white pepper gravy, as I remember it.)

After lunch we were married, on the twenty-sixth day of January in nineteen forty-one. We drove on to Lander, Wyoming, where we checked into a little hotel on Main Street. It had a bar downstairs, and like most such places in Wyoming, country western music played into the early hours of the morning. I had my first alcoholic drink there. As a young Baptist I had signed a pledge, at the end of an evangelistic rally at youth camp, that I would never drink alcohol. My feeling as I drank that beverage was that I was trading my salvation for the taste of whiskey, but then — I was in love — I could deal with another blot — a big one! — later.

After a couple of days, Pete left me in town with an aunt and went to his parents' ranch to start working as a cowboy for his father. Percy raised purebred Hereford cattle. He and Esther, Pete's mother, owned a place on the Wind River, and leased grazing land from the Bureau of Indian Affairs.

Chapter 12

One day early in February, Pete's aunt drove me to the ranch. It was so cold in Lander that the smoke from chimneys hung inertly in the air above the houses. It was a day that hair around my face turned white with frost, and my nostrils froze shut. We drove up-country on icy roads. When we arrived at the ranch the kitchen door was open and the sun was shining. Esther was baking bread. I thought, "Boy, the weather sure changes fast in this country!"

"So this is my new sister!" A blue-eyed, sandy-haired, freckle-faced boy of eleven or twelve was sitting at the kitchen table eating biscuits and syrup. He had the sweetest smile, and I loved him from that day forever. He was Jack, Pete's younger brother. Esther was kneading a huge pillow of dough on the other side of the table. She looked at me for what seemed like a very long time, and then she smiled. A bird sang outside the door. Everything seemed easy and pleasant. I had finally met Pete's mother and Jack. There would still be his sister Laura, and Percy, but the prospect didn't seem so frightening as it had.

Aunt Doll drove me back to town. As we neared Lander, I realized that the temperature had not changed since we left there that morning. Smoke was still lying motionless over the housetops and it was, if anything, even colder.

I fell in love with the "upper country." In my mind the upper country began just north of Rawlins at Muddy Gap, and took up the whole of the Sweetwater, went through Lander and up to Crowheart and Burris. Crowheart postoffice was and is still a little white store and filling station sitting beneath Crowheart Butte, atop which Chief Washakie, chief of the Shoshones, was purported to have killed a Crow chief and brandished his heart on his spear. Some of the stories claimed he ate the heart to attain the Crow chief's courage, but I never quite believed it. Several miles up the road from Crowheart nestled a little log postoffice which was Burris.

"Do you like milk?" Percy asked me. I had just moved up to the ranch to be with Pete. We were at the supper table. Trying to be cute and funny, and impress the father-in-law I had met only hours before, I said, "Yes, just like a calf likes milk." "Take her to the corral and tie her in with the cow, Pete," said Percy.

49

There was real, thick cream on the table. Esther had cooked dried apricots with sugar and cinnamon. The combination was one of the greatest desserts I had ever tasted. The cream on that ranch was scooped off the pans of fresh milk. I learned that the milk would be left in the flat pans to sour or "clabber" and then the cream saved to churn for butter. The clabbered milk was placed into cloth salt sacks and hung out on the clothesline to drip. This made cottage cheese. It had a texture that the manufactured kind never equals.

One spring evening on the ranch Laura, home from school, and Jack and I were sitting on the davenport in the ranchhouse living room in the dusk. The sun had gone down and we had not yet lighted the gas lamp. (It would be years before electricity would reach the upper country.) Jack studied me for a few minutes and then said, seriously, "You sure are pretty in the dark."

When Jack entered the seventh grade he had to go to Lander for school. He had a pet pig at home, named Pinky. Pinky had for a long time had the run of the house. Frequently he could be found asleep in Esther's wicker basket of clothes to be ironed, which got him in trouble even though Jack maintained that Pinky was a clean pig. One weekend Jack came home and arrived at the house in time for supper. One dish was a big platter of pork chops. When it was passed to Jack, he paled. "Is this Pinky?" he asked. When the answer was affirmative, Jack pushed the platter away. "I'd feel just like a cannibal if I ate Pinky," he choked, with tears in his eyes.

At the ranch the outhouse was several yards down the hill from the house. Unaccustomed to an outdoor facility, especially since that one seemed uncomfortably isolated, I always waited until I was desperate to make that trek. I knew there was livestock and God knows what else between the house and that little two-hole shack.

Within a couple of months of living on that ranch with Pete's family, I developed a bladder infection. It was partly due to my reluctance to use the outhouse, and partly due to the rich cream and milk and other great ranch foods. Esther drove me to Lander to see the doctor. He examined me, prescribed some medicine, and said, "You know you are pregnant, don't you?" Well, I did, but I had not come to terms with that reality. "When did you have your last period?" he asked. I could not remember, but he said he thought I would deliver in September or October.

While Pete worked for Percy, he and I slept in the bunkhouse and ate with the family. I was getting fairly large and uncomfortable and a little homesick. One evening, just after dark, I made my way past the corrals and down to the outhouse. As I came back, I heard what I thought was the family dog, Willkie, barking and yipping and howling out in the alfalfa field. I ran in and breathlessly reported,

"Something's the matter with Willkie, way out in the field!" Everybody, including Willkie, who was curled up alongside the kitchen stove, stared at me. Then they all howled with glee, and I learned that there were coyotes in that country.

Soon I was getting too big to get around easily, and it was decided that I needed to go to the hospital at Fort Washakie and bide my time until the baby would make its appearance. Fort Washakie was the tribal and Bureau of Indian Affairs headquarters for the Shoshone and Arapaho tribes who shared the reservation. It was also the location of the Indian hospital. Pete was three thirty-seconds Shoshone on his mother's side, and was entitled to treatment at the Indian hospital. Assorted relatives visited me there while I spent what seemed like an eternity in a little side room.

One day my water broke. A nurse informed me what that meant. This happened to be a day when Percy and Esther stopped by on their way home from Lander. Percy had had a few beers and was feeling clever. I was having labor pains about every ten minutes and was, at the nurse's recommendation, pacing the halls in my nightgown. From time to time I was getting nauseous and rushing to the bathroom to throw up. When Esther told Percy about this part of it, Percy cocked one eyebrow at me and said, "That's not how you do it. It has to get out the way it got in." The humor of that escaped me. I wasn't yet inured to a cowman's way of looking at things.

Chapter 13

My baby son, Preston Lee, made his appearance early the next morning, and Pete and a friend, Red, came to see me in the afternoon. Red was carrying a bouquet of flowers, and came over eagerly to see the squirming little person I held. Pete hung back, seeming a little embarrassed to have fathered this child. Naturally, the nurse took the baby from my arms and handed him over to Red, saying, "Aren't you proud of your wife? She did such a good job!" Red stepped back, his flaming face matching his red hair. Then he paled so much that his many freckles seemed to stand out from his face. The two men soon left, after Red shared his philosophy with Pete. "I tell you, Pete, you always have to look after the women and the little boogers."

Preston was three months old when I thought I had to go home and show him to Mom and Dad. Esther drove me to Lander. My baby and I got on a bus bound for Laramie, where I planned to visit

Darolyn and catch a ride with my Dad, who was still working at the tie plant in Laramie and commuting to the farm in Colorado.

Dad picked Darolyn and me up on his day off. We were a few miles into Colorado when Dad commented that the area was all "dry land farming." Darolyn asked him seriously, "Well, what do they do when it rains?" With a straight face, Dad explained, "They have these gigantic tarps they spread out to keep the fields from getting wet." I laughed. Darolyn said, "Oh."

Mom and Dad and the boys and Dora were all glad to make the acquaintance of little Preston. They tossed him around and fed him vanilla wafers and ginger snaps, and he entertained them. He had just learned to sit up, and had a perpetual smile and chuckled delightedly at all the attention he got.

Darolyn rode back to Laramie with Dad. Before he left, he said to me that I was welcome to visit, but I shouldn't even be **thinking** about moving back home. Well, I wasn't. "You've made your choice, Sis," Dad said, not unkindly. "Now it's up to you to do your best with it." I firmly planned to. My vacation there would be over in a couple of weeks, and I would be returning to the ranch and Pete.

It was a beautiful green and gold Sunday afternoon in December. Howard and Richard and I had gone for a long walk up the country road. I mentioned to them for about the tenth time that I had this feeling that "something is going to happen." We had just come into the house when we heard on the radio, "Pearl Harbor has just been bombed by the Japanese." A dark shadow had fallen over our lives.

Within a few days, Pete came down on a bus from Wyoming, carrying a sheaf of papers for me to sign. He intended to enlist, but as a married man and a father, he had to get me to agree. Certain that he would hate me forever if I resisted, I signed the papers. Pete and I and Preston Lee spent the next month on the farm with my family, waiting for him to be called. By the time the call came for him to report, I was pregnant with my next baby. Preston was just four and a half months old.

We had Christmas with the family. It was a bittersweet time. Finally, Pete was called up, and we took him to the bus station and he was gone. I went back to the ranch around the middle of February, and Carol Ann was born at the end of September. When she was a month old, I got on a crowded Greyhound bus headed back to Colorado. With a tiny baby in my arms and a fourteen month old toddler at my side, we went "home to Mom and Dad."

Dad told me, "You need to get a job. Your mother will take care of the babies and you can give us your allotment check." I applied at the Fort Collins Express-Courier, telling the editor that I had had

55

newspaper experience and was sure I could do anything they needed. I was hired. I filed proofs, answered the phone, and was eventually allowed to take want-ads. I loved the atmosphere at the paper. I even had hopes of being sent out on a story with one of the reporters some day.

Red Moffett, editor of the paper, told me that the war would last a minimum of four years but that we would win it. "Well, if I thought it was going to be that long, I think I'd shoot myself now," I said. His smile was indulgent. I was twenty years old. It did last four years, and I did not shoot myself.

Chapter 14

Pete came home on furlough in the spring. He begged me to take Preston and Carol Ann and go back to the ranch. I was not enthusiastic, but Dad and Mom both argued for him. "He is a serviceman," they told me. "He should have peace of mind while he is overseas, and if that is what it takes, you should go." I think Mom was pretty tired, anyway. Toad and Bob had both enlisted, Toad in the army infantry and Bob in the navy. With the big boys gone and Dad still working in Laramie, Mom had a lot to do on the farm.

I went back to the ranch and spent several months with Percy and Esther, but then I felt the need to be doing something. Pete was home on leave once again, and then was sent to Camp Polk, Louisiana. His legs were badly burned when a campfire got out of control on a bivouac. We thought he might be sent home after six months in a hospital, but instead he was put on a ship and sent to England. He spent some time in a hospital there, and then was released in time to join his field artillery battalion just before they crossed the vital bridge at Remagen, Germany.

Soon after Pete went overseas I went to Laramie to find a job. War was hell for the soldiers in Europe and in the Pacific, but it was monotony on the home front. Money was good, though, for those of us who took war-time jobs usually held by men. I went to work for the Union Pacific railroad, checking west-bound freight trains. It was a fearful job. The first night I was there a yard man came in carrying a bloody shoe. A hobo had been killed trying to jump into a moving boxcar.

Most of the work involved walking the length of the long freight trains, checking to see that the order of the cars jibed with the manifests with which they had come in. Sometimes cars had been taken out of the train and others added. This was important information if the cars were to reach their destination.

We women checkers found the job to be hard, dirty and dangerous. Sometimes the train would start to move long before the check was finished. On a couple of occasions I found myself caught between two trains moving in opposite directions on either side of me. It was so dizzy-making I had to lie down until at least one of the trains had passed.

Frequently one long train would block the checker from the one that was to be checked, which necessitated a long walk around the blocking train and back to the train to be checked. Those trains were long. There was one quick, if hazardous, solution. It involved jumping on the coupling between two cars on the blocking train, and swinging down on the other side. This was a practice frowned upon by the Union Pacific. If, God forbid, the train started to move while you teetered between the two cars, you could be thrown under the train. I didn't do that foolish trick often.

While I was working in Laramie, the children and I lived in an apartment owned by a couple who befriended us. During our stay there I celebrated my twenty-first birthday. Jess and Viola loved my children, and Viola tended them while I worked. Viola became a caring and loyal friend to me. My life has been blessed with this friendship. It is said that a person has been blessed to have one true friend. I have been doubly blessed to have two friends, Viola and Darolyn, who have always loved me, no matter what.

Always on the brink of panic, I stayed with the Union Pacific until Pete was discharged. He arrived one night at the apartment where the children and I were living. It was with a great sense of relief that I left that job and Pete and I and our two children went back to the ranch. The atom bomb had been dropped on Hiroshima and Nagasaki, and the war was over. We could begin our married life with hope for the future. An alien force had entered the world bringing a new fear, but as we moved to the upper country, the atomic threat seemed to be an anxiety we could ignore. However, there would be another kind of anxiety to hover over our lives.

Chapter 15

I grew to love Pete's family, and especially Esther. She was an exemplary woman, to me. Her children adored her and depended on her. Percy relied on her for all kinds of support; she kept house, cooked, did laundry and helped with moving cattle, branding and all the outdoors things a ranchwoman is called upon to do. Esther was the first person I remember showing me affection. She put her arms around me one day when I was doing dishes at the ranch. Her hug surprised me.

Esther was an imposing woman, a person of great dignity and maturity. She was three-sixteenths Shoshone, and had gone to an Indian school as a young girl. Though I didn't think about it at the time, I came to realize later that she was a Christian of deep faith. She sometimes questioned me about my faith and asked me to sing some of the hymns I had learned in Baptist Sunday school. She read her Bible often in the evenings, sitting in her rocking chair in the light of the gas lamp.

Esther had leased a three hundred and twenty acre place with a big stone abandoned house on it, on the Wind River Indian Reservation. This was winter pasture for a bunch of white-face cows. Percy moved Pete and me and our two children down to the "Bain place," as it was called. The house had been built by an easterner named Mosely for a summer home, but his wife had taken one look at it and said, "Huh-Unn!" So it was sold to Tom Bain and his wife, who lived there for a few years until a flash flood came down the sand draw alongside the place, and flooded it, filling the basement of the house and a good part of the barn with silt. At that point, the Bains moved out and sold the place to the reservation.

The Bain place was on the wrong side of the east fork of the Wind River. It could only be reached by way of a trolley, a little box pulled across the river on a heavy cable, hand over hand. The house was a marvel made of a pinkish beige color quarry stone cut in huge blocks. Window sills were a foot deep. Two large bay windows fronted the south side of the house, and there were fireplaces in several rooms. And the outhouse was the fanciest in the country. It even had a little one-hole seat for children. The house had only been a sort of winter cow camp for Percy and Esther, though, and was furnished with only a few sticks of furniture; chairs without backs, an old round oak table, a cupboard with curtains in the place of doors, and a double bed. The kitchen also had an old Majestic range for cooking. It was a hazard for the cook, because the door to the firebox was prone to fall off the stove at odd hours.

The bay window in the kitchen of the Bain house looked out across a long meadow to a mountain which seemed very close in the summer when it was shadowed with green and blue, and its contours were soft, and very far away in the winter when it turned white with blue shadows, sharply defined. It was always a lovely view, no matter what the season.

The Bain place was a wonderful place for children. They were free to run and play over acres of meadows and hillsides, river bank and woods. They discovered where the rabbits and ravens nested and raised their young. They saw deer and elk and moose feeding in the long meadow below the house. For them, as well as for me, nature held countless wonders to observe and marvel over; the always-moving air, air you could taste and smell and feel, air in which the coming weather could be sensed.

We had cats and dogs, horses and cows. And there were chickens who lived with us from time to time; chickens who had names; "Squatty," who swallowed a shoestring and finally died of it, "Eggatha," who inadvertently spent a week under a washtub in the back yard and emerged a skinny fowl but none the worse for the experience, "Waddly," Carol's pet hen who was short and stout and swallowed a fishline, hook and all, which Carol managed to extricate without doing permanent damage, and Preston's pet, "Cutie Pie," who was a tall, slender and elegant hen. We also had a pet magpie, appropriately named Maggie. She strutted up and down the window sill like the queen of birds, and entertained us with her arrogant demeanor.

As soon as we got settled at the Bain place, I began thinking that we should have another baby. Pete had not had the joy of seeing Preston and Carol through their baby years, and I thought he should have that experience. He was not enthusiastic, but within the year, Daniel Richard was born at the hospital at Fort Washakie. We brought him home swaddled in blankets on a snowy day in December, crossing the river in the box of the trolley. I was nervous, afraid he would slip out of his cocoon of blankets and fall into the icy water below.

Three years later, the baby Janet Susan, "Susie" was born. We had our four children. My ideal of a family. Two boys and two girls. Each of my girls had a big brother. When Pete was home I was filled with satisfaction, peace and contentment.

One Easter Sunday some friends came up and had dinner with us at the Bain place. As they were leaving, we all stood in front of the house. It was warm and damp, and was beginning to snow, large, clinging flakes. "Well, one thing; when a storm comes this time of year, you know it isn't going to last long," I thought.

By the time it stopped snowing two days and nights later, there were thirty-six inches of snow on the ground. We had planned to go to town in a day or so to stock up on groceries. We ran out of everything except pinto beans. No fat, no meat, and worst of all, no salt. Pinto beans cooked in water, unseasoned, make poor eating.

Pete stepped on a nail in the early part of the week while we were snowed in at the Bain place. His foot became infected and swollen. The woodpile was buried under three feet of snow. Wading through snow to the river to carry water, and then digging out and chopping wood to keep a fire going became a major job, and there was nobody there to do it but me. We finally got through the week, however, and shoveling our way, we managed to get to the pickup on the other side of the river and go to town.

Our first stop in town was at the Cowboy Cafe for lots of bacon and eggs and pancakes. Two hungry children ate as if they had never had food before; as a matter of fact, the only sound at our table was that of clinking silverware until we had all filled our stomachs to capacity.

Generally we had venison or elk meat at the Bain place; the wild life was plentiful right along the river. But once in a while we ran out, and ate beans and potatoes for a while. When we had meat, it was suspended from the roof of the barn when the weather was cool, or wrapped in a tarp with a lot of salt in the basement of the house when it was too warm to hang it out. Magpies and flies were always a problem we had to take into account. Also, meat tends to dry into a kind of jerky as it is kept, so the dried part has to be trimmed off.

We never bought dog food or cat food. Our dogs ate the trimmings from the deer or elk meat, and the pancakes I cooked extra for them at breakfast. Our cats were on their own. They caught their own food, and we supplemented it with a little milk if we had it.

Chapter 16

In the summer we went to cow camp. This involved packing tent, ·
bedrolls, food and a couple of changes of clothing for each of us.
Some summers we had the luxury of a sheepwagon. Cooking
supplies and food were stowed in handy drawers and shelves under
the bunk, and food was cooked on a camp stove and eaten at a small
fold-out table alongside the built-in bunk. When we had the
sheepwagon the children snuggled together in the bunk, except for the
baby, who slept cozily in a drawer near the stove. Pete and I slept in
the tent just outside the sheepwagon.

Most summers, though, we had only the tent. Then I cooked
squatting on my heels over a log campfire. We all slept outside in our
bedrolls on cushiony, fragrant mattresses of pine boughs. I would try
to stay awake to watch the movement of the stars across the sky, only
to drop off into a deep and dreamless sleep. The bellowing of the
bulls far off, and the sound of the horse bells as the horses grazed

around us was a familiar and beloved music. The fathomless black of the night sky, with stars seeming to be suspended brilliantly above us, was a glorious sight. It was cold at night in these high mountain meadows. The warm bedroll was comfortable. And near us the children slept peacefully.

Rising at dawn with dew, or sometimes frost, on the tarpaulin over the bedrolls, washing in the icy mountain stream, shivering in the morning breeze as we waited for the water to boil for coffee, and then frying bacon and eggs in an iron skillet over the campfire, all this made a body feel intensely alive, all the senses aware. It was both peaceful and challenging.

Sometimes in the early dusk of a summer evening in cow camp, we climbed to the top of a cliff behind the camp to watch the stars come out in the afterglow of the sunset and to listen to the sound of the wind through the wings of the bullbats or nighthawks as they made deep dives and pull-ups chasing mosquitoes and other night-flying insects. The rush of the air against their wings when they pull out of their dives is a unique and marvelous sound.

Even though life on the mountains in the summer with the cattle was physically demanding, with water to carry in buckets up a hill from the creek, wood to gather and chop, and fires to build and maintain, it was still pretty much like normal ranch life. Except that cow camp was more uncomfortable in some ways. Sitting on the heels to rest or to cook is tiring and hard on the back. Bathing in a mountain stream is shockingly icy, and washing the hair in it brings on a terrible, if short-lived, headache. Doing laundry in a dishpan of cold water and wringing it out by hand, and draping it over sagebrush or barbed wire to dry, is a real chore.

Nevertheless, we loved it. Some summers our camp was in the highest mountain meadows from the middle of June until the end of August, with days of sunshine and days of rain and fog. We could climb up a rocky cliff and see for miles, as far as the Grand Tetons on a clear day.

One day a few months before Susie was born, we decided that Pete would go to town and pick up supplies, and I would walk down hill for a couple of miles with the children. Jack would meet us at a designated spot in the ranch pickup and take us to Percy's ranch. Danny was only eighteen months old. I carried him, and Preston and Carol took turns dragging a gunny-sack of laundry to do at the ranch house.

We took a wrong turn on the trail, and we walked and walked. There was no sign of Jack. Thunderheads were roiling up on the horizon and the noonday sun was hot. We were hungry. Occasionally there were wild currant and gooseberry bushes along the trail, so we stopped and picked handfuls to eat. Finally at mid-afternoon, Pete met us in the pickup. Jack, having missed us, had gone back to the ranch in a panic. He reported that there was a trail of something being dragged at one spot where he stopped. He guessed that a bear had been dragging something along, and he was afraid that it might be one of us. Pete asked him what he thought could have become of the rest of us.

I never saw a bear while we were in that camp, but a young couple who were honeymooning after having run away to elope, had encountered a black bear near our camp some time before. I wasn't afraid of seeing one. I had heard a wolf howl one night at the Bain place, and the scream of a mountain lion was not an uncommon sound.

Chapter 17

Horses and cattle made up a big part of what occupied us while we lived at the Bain place. I was never a lover of horses. That is, I did like the smell of their sun-warmed hides. I could pat their noses and jaws, and could occasionally lead one to water when the occasion demanded, always conscious of their hooves getting dangerously close to my heels. Under duress I could, with help, mount one of the older and more dependable horses, if that were the only way of getting to where I needed to be.

For a time there was a high-spirited, blooded young stallion kept in our meadow. I was terrified of him. He was a beautiful animal, a palomino of perfect proportions. I could appreciate the perfection of his color and form, but when, as he often did, he came pounding up from the pasture with his head raised high and came right through our back yard, twisting and bucking and kicking up his heels, he scared me almost witless.

There were memorable experiences with horses, one of the most memorable ones took place in the late evening one year in the month of July. Pete had been working for the neighboring Double Diamond ranch and away from home for a month or so. He and the other cowhands were holding cattle on summer range in an area around Lake of the Woods, high up in the mountains. As a special treat, Pete was taking me up to the cow camp for a week, over the Independence Day holiday, July fourth. He had arranged for the children to stay with Percy and Esther. Another cowhand's wife would be at the camp, and we would be company for one another while our husbands moved cattle from one grassy meadow to another.

By the time supplies were bought at the general store in town and loaded in the panniers on a packhorse called "Mooney," it was around nine o'clock in the evening, and getting dark. Pete and the other man had managed a few beers at a bar near the store, and had bought a bottle of something or other. They put me on the widest horse I had ever seen. He was appropriately called "Beer Belly." I was wearing a light leather jacket and no gloves. As darkness descended so did the temperature. As we climbed, it grew progressively colder. I couldn't see where we were going. The two men got further and further ahead, and I could hear them laughing and joking as they shared the bottle they had bought.

This went on for what seemed hours, but when we were about halfway to our destination, Beer Belly finally came alive and realized that he was on the way back to the cow camp corrals and his hay and oats. And all of a sudden, we were galloping along a narrow trail through dense forest. Branches slapped my face and pulled my hair, catching the fringe on my sleeves, and the worst of it was that I couldn't see them coming. At the last, I sensed that we were descending a steep shale slope, with Beer Belly sitting on his haunches and sliding.

When we finally got to the camp and I slid off Beer Belly's back, my legs felt about two inches long. That is a phenomenon I never quite figured out. My calves were bruised and rubbed raw. It was not an experience designed to make me an enthusiast.

Actually, Pete and Carol and Preston called me "Mom, the dude," because from the time we left the corral on the rare occasions I managed the nerve to get on a horse, my mount either tried to stop and graze, or turned and headed back for the corral. Pete was not patient: his attitude was, "Damn it, make that horse behave, and stay up with us!"

Once when I was allowed to "help" move some yearlings up country about ten miles, the horse I was on was being lazy. The calves were getting into the trees and brush along the trail. Pete rode

73

up behind me and gave my horse a solid smack on the rump with his reins. "Flax, damn it, get to work!" I almost fell off old Flax as he leaped forward. My stirrups were never short enough to give me a footing. Once, riding into a hunting camp where I cooked for forty-one days one fall, my horse gave a little jump as we headed down a creek bank. "Pete, I'm going to fall off," I fussed as I lost a stirrup and began sliding forward on the horse's neck. "You can't fall off," Pete informed me, just as I went head over heels and somersaulted down the bank and into the creek.

Chapter 18

Living with cattle was always a mixed blessing. Ours were Herefords, red with white faces. Early spring brought new calves, clean and sparkling in the sunshine, and I loved seeing them leap and frolic in the meadows as their mothers grazed. But I was always nervous, and felt there was an element of danger in being around the cattle.

One February day we were in the midst of a warm spell brought on by a chinook. Pete decided to bring some hay from the meadow up to the barn. He hitched up the team and wagon. The children and I were instructed to get on top of the hay and trample it down as he pitched it up from the stack.

It was a pleasant day's occupation in the warmth of the sun. After several hours, Pete said to me, "Go on up to the house and put on a pot of coffee, and we will take this load up to the barn."

Obediently I jumped off the wagon and accompanied by Patches, our little cow dog, started up through the meadow. A young heifer with a brand new calf looked up and saw Patches, and made a wild-eyed dash at her. Patches dodged and made a bee line for the house, and the heifer turned on me. Luckily for me, my legs needed no instruction! I was into the barn, through it, out the back and at the house before I even had time to think about it.

Our red pickup truck had several dents on both sides from occasions when we had some bulls in the meadow at the Bain place waiting for their annual spring trek to summer range in the mountains. These bulls were cranky with their seasonal infusion of testosterone in Nature's faithful preparation for the mating season. Each bull took issue with the presence of other bulls in the meadow. A great deal of bellowing and rushing at each other took place, and sometimes, with the pickup parked along the road to the house, it took several hits in the midst of their fussing.

To encourage the cattle to eat the rough grass in the meadow and to supplement its value as food, we carried "oil cake" in buckets and scattered it in the grass. Actually, when he was at home, Pete fed it from the pickup. When he was away, it was my job to fill a couple of coal scuttles with the cake and carry it out about an eighth of a mile and scatter it. Predictably, the cows crowded and shoved behind me as they followed their feed. This was not my favorite job as a ranch housewife. As I prolonged my morning coffee after breakfast, the whitefaces gathered outside the kitchen bay window and rolled their eyes reproachfully.

The first cow in line as I started out each morning was not a whiteface. She was a black and white milk cow we called "Old Bawley" because she bawled the whole way out to the edge of the meadow. She was enormous, and was right at my heels, bawling in my ear and slobbering on my shoulder. I had been assured that she was a gentle old cow, and she was. Nevertheless, there was a certain discomfort in feeling her proximity to my back. I struggled to maintain a leisurely stroll, lest the whole bovine group break into a gallop and run over me.

Bawley had a calf, the cutest little Disney-like critter with enormous brown eyes and long, thick lashes. Pete decided that we didn't need another milk cow, and that it was time to take the calf to the butcher. I hated the idea, but we could use the meat. We got as far as the gate. I got out to open and close the gate as we went through. But it was not possible to get back into the pickup without a glimpse of those limpid eyes gazing at me.

"Oh, for God's sake," Pete said grumpily when he saw the tears on my face. However, he turned the pickup around, I reopened the gate, and we drove back to the barn with Bawley's calf. We never did eat her. She eventually joined the herd and finally replaced her mother as the family milk cow.

Chapter 19

Life on the reservation, in comparison with the way I grew up, was full and exceedingly interesting. One person I came to know and love was Pete's grandmother, whom everyone knew as "Betty." Betty was three-eighths Shoshone. She had a round face and snapping brown eyes, and wore her graying hair in two braids down her back. She was married to Grandpa John, a respected rancher, and they had a prosperous life on the reservation. Grandma Betty could speak both English and the language of the tribe so she was much in demand during political campaigns of national and state as well as local politicians.

When I was pregnant with my second child and Pete was going with Percy and Esther, taking the cattle to sell in the Omaha stockyards, I stayed with the grandparents on their ranch because it was necessary for me to be closer to the hospital. I enjoyed the visit. After supper every night, Betty and John would turn off the kitchen lights and sit near the kitchen range. They both chewed tobacco, and I remember the sizzle as they spit into the flames of the stove. I can still see the firelight flickering on the walls and ceiling, and hear Grandpa John chuckle as they talked.

One day a local politician and merchant who Betty knew and liked came to call. It was mid-afternoon and Betty was sitting in a large, overstuffed armchair smoking a pipe when the man drove into the yard. "Good God, I don't want him to see me smoking," she grumbled, slipping her pipe unter the cushion of her chair. While Betty and the caller visited, I was extremely nervous, expecting to see smoke curling up from under the cushion. Finally he left, and Grandma Betty rescued her pipe.

Betty's doctor informed her one day that she had high blood pressure. He recommended that she eat less, and also should avoid eating fat foods. The same night, Betty cooked up a big platter of pork chops. Filling her plate at dinner, she said as she stabbed two large chops, "No damned doctor is going to tell me what I can eat!"

The Bain place was the sobering-up place for several of Pete's drinking cronies. Different ones came to stay for varying lengths of time. Shorty was one of my favorites. He worked on ranches as wrangler or cook all summer, drank all fall, and then came to our place with Pete to sober up and get well. Shorty was a rotund, jolly-faced, whiskery man a little over five feet tall, and somewhat crippled. He was a wonderful cook. When he came to the Bain place to recuperate, he initially disappeared into the back bedroom which we kept for just such occasions.

For several days Shorty holed up, coming out only for a cup of coffee. This he would have to hold with both trembling hands. He would drink as much of it as he could get to his mouth. Then he would disappear into his room again.

At last, some morning when he felt well, Shorty would emerge from the room, wash up and shave, and then take over the kitchen. Pete wasn't much for chopping wood, and Shorty would mumble curses as he cut wood and kindling and carried it to build a handy woodpile in the back entryway. Then he would take apart the big cookstove, take down the stovepipe, clean out all the soot and ashes, and blacken the stove with stove polish. And I could forget the kitchen until spring.

Susie, our unexpected but precious baby, was about eighteen months old the last time or two Shorty came to stay with us. Every day as he cooked, Shorty would put little lumps of brown sugar at the edge of the kitchen table where Susie could just reach it by stretching as far as her chubby little arms could reach. Shorty loved this curly-headed urchin. He enjoyed watching her play. Needless to say, she loved him and his brown sugar, too.

Some of the best Swiss steak I have ever eaten came out of that kitchen when Shorty cooked. He pounded the meat, usually elk, sometimes moose. (Rarely beef. We couldn't afford to eat our livestock.) He floured the meat when it was tenderized enough to suit him, and seared it in a big cast-iron roaster, seasoned it with salt and pepper, added potatoes and onions. It was always delicious and appreciated.

Jersey was another character who was in and out of our house during those years. Rumor had it that Jersey had been an important figure in professional prize-fighting circles and also in some aspects of horse racing before moving out west. Whatever his background, he was extremely knowledgeable in those areas and could cite statistics, facts and gossip around those and related topics.

Jersey was a most sentimental man. Women and children brought forth his deepest sentiments. He often drank to excess. On one of his sprees, after he had been drinking in town for several days, he was seen walking up the street with tears streaming down his cheeks. One of his friends from the saloon asked him, "What's the matter, Jersey? Somebody dead?"

Several days earlier at our house, Jersey had commented on the good looks of our children and their exemplary manners toward their elders. Pete and I smiled and told Jersey that we thought we had done such a good job with our first four that we intended to have a dozen.

"My God," Jersey hiccupped, "those people told me they were going to have twelve kids. How in the hell will they feed that many mouths? Old Pete will work himself to death. I say, that poor cowboy will work himself to death!"

Jersey was a great story-teller. He told us once of riding up to a cabin on a ranch far up in the mountains and finding the wife of the young rancher in labor. She was alone, her husband having ridden to get a neighbor woman to assist with the birth. Jersey himself had to be the midwife, the birth being imminent. The only thing he could find to wrap the newborn in was some cotton. "When they unwrapped it, that little thing looked just like a gosling, it did," Jersey reported enthusiastically. "I say, with all that cotton sticking to it, it looked just like a gosling!"

Jersey kept himself meticulously clean. About once a week while he was with us, we had to turn the kitchen over to him for half a day while he heated bath water and took his weekly wash-tub bath. Jersey shaved every day as well. That was unusual for those men who visited us. They were all interesting people, and I grew fond of each of them.

Bunny was one of my favorites. He was an old time cow hand and rodeo rider. Many times I watched him sit on a skittish half-broke horse and visit with us as we sat in our pick-up. Bunny's horse would be doing a little quick-step dance, while Bunny opened his sack of Bull Durham with his teeth, poured tobacco into a cigarette paper and rolled and lighted his smoke, all with one hand, while keeping a tight rein on the bronco with the other.

Bunny, like most of these men, was a bachelor. Pete and I were at his cabin one day at meal time. He insisted that we eat with him. He washed his hands in the wash basin, threw his wash water out the back door, and then filled the basin with flour and mixed a batch of baking powder biscuits in it. It was easier not to notice. Hunger had taught us to overlook a lot.

Once Bunny rode in to spend a night with us. In the middle of the night I woke to hear someone moving around in the house and dipping water from the pail in the kitchen. Then I heard hurried footsteps. This went on for a few minutes. Then quieted. I went back to sleep and thought no more about it. Next morning I was surprised to find that Bunny had mounted his horse and ridden away. Later I went to change the sheets on his bed. When I turned back the blanket I found the explanation for his hurried departure. Smoking in bed, he had set the sheet and mattress afire. There was a sizable charred and soaking wet hole down into the mattress. It was a while before we saw Bunny again. I was sorry, though. I was fonder of him than I was of any piece of bedding we owned.

Another sometime visitor I grew to love was Prentiss. Prentiss was a marvelous sourdough cook. He could make the best pancakes, biscuits and light bread from that sourdough. He could even make a wonderful raisin spice cake with it. He tried a few times to help me get a start with the stuff, but my sourdough starter only lived a few weeks. It sort of separated and all the flour and solid material settled into the bottom of the crock. A sour smelling kind of liquid stayed on the top. The whole mess was a discouragement to me. And Prentiss remarked seriously that he thought women were congenitally incapable of grasping the fundamentals of sourdough baking. He and I gave up on the project at about the same time.

Prentiss did some trapping along the river when he stayed with us at the Bain place. Watching him prepare beaver pelts, I learned a lot about how the fur was made usable. Prentiss never took more from nature than he gave back, one way or another, and I found his process of scraping the hides and mounting them on boards to dry an interesting project.

85

Prentiss was quite deaf. At one St. Patrick's Day celebration in town everyone had imbibed freely for several hours when a brouhaha broke out in the saloon where the crowd was gathered. A couple of local cowhands had offended one another, and they proceeded to the street in front of the saloon to settle matters between themselves, with a sizable crowd observing. Half a dozen punches were more or less landed in the melee that ensued, and then hands were shaken and the crowd returned to the saloon for drinks all around.

"Where's Prentiss?" somebody asked. He was nowhere to be found until someone went out to start his car and go home. Seeing a dusty pair of cowboy boots sticking out from under a pickup truck, he investigated. It was Prentiss. In his efforts to hear what was going on, he had stuck his chin a little too close to the fracas and taken a knockout punch. Revived, he spend the rest of the celebration sitting in a corner booth, scratching his head and muttering irritably.

"Little Bill" was a tall and lanky horse trader who came and stayed with us at the Bain place for varying periods of time. He, too, was a wonderful raconteur. He kept us entertained during many long winter evenings around the kitchen stove. The only thing was, when he stayed with us, in October he took a bath in our wash tub behind the stove. Then he put on all new clothes and wore them all winter. There were several layers; long heavy underwear, Levi jeans, blue chambrey shirt, and then layers and layers of flannel shirts which were donned one by one as the weather grew colder. We believed that he wore all these things even to bed. He tended to ripen as the winter wore on, and we tended to move further and further back from the stove. Bill had twinkling eyes and long, yellow teeth. We enjoyed his visits.

Little Bill had been struck by lightning while riding horseback with another man on a ranch up the country from us. The other rider was killed, as were both horses. Bill suffered from periodic spells of internal bleeding as a result of the lightning strike. During these spells, Bill's complexion became a waxy yellow, and he became exceedingly nervous, spilling tobacco as he tried to roll cigarettes with his long, shaking fingers. One morning Bill was in the kitchen waiting for the coffee to finish percolating. I was cooking breakfast, and Bill accidentally happened to bump a box of baby magpies Preston had rescued and brought into the house. A cacaphony of squawks made Bill jump and scatter a paper full of tobacco. He didn't say a word, just walked jerkily out of the kitchen. He walked around and around outside for a while and then disappeared into his room for the rest of the morning. By the time for the noon meal he had recovered, and he never did mention the incident.

Our life on the Bain place was light and shadow. The beauty of the freshness of the mornings, the ever-moving clouds and sunshine, was a joy for me. On the other hand, Pete was often gone for days at a time. Sometimes this was necessary in the business of the ranch. Sometimes it was a drinking binge. I was contented when he was at home. When he was gone I was nervous. We were isolated; the nearest neighbors at least six miles upriver from us. Sometimes when the weather was warm I put on my dressiest clothes, dressed up the children, and we walked the quarter of a mile to the river. We sat on the bank and watched the sparkling water, and once we saw a family of otters sliding down a muddy slide they had made on the bank. Once in a while we would see a car moving along the road on the other side of the river, a mile away.

When the river was frozen over, Preston and Carol could cross on the ice and wait for the school bus up near the road. Pete would walk with them and build them a small sagebrush fire in a more or less sheltered spot. This made me terribly nervous. Especially so, when one day, the school bus failed to come for them, and Carol Ann's hands were frostbitten. She cried in the night from the pain, and I was helplessly angry for the careless way in which they had been left for hours, she and Preston calling for us until Pete finally heard them and went to pick them up. We had no telephone, so the teacher/bus driver had no way to let us know she was not coming. And Preston and Carol had no way of knowing, either. So they waited.

When the river was low in the summer, we could park the pickup on the other side and wade across. We could drive to town and spend a day shopping and visiting with friends. One day we decided to go to Lander, some sixty miles away. We got dressed, and Pete began carrying the children across; Preston, then Carol Ann, and finally, Danny. Susie had not yet been born. I remember the day vividly; the sun shone and the water sparkled. I was excited to be going to town.

I was carrying Pete's good shoes and clean socks, and my own nylon hose and dressy shoes. Suddenly I slipped on a smooth rock in the river, and sat up to my armpits in icy water. And Pete's shoes were bobbing along, headed downstream. "God damn it, Allyene, can't you do **anything** right?" Pete shouted, as he raced along the bank and finally caught them. It was a little disconcerting to be yelled at, since I would be spending the day in a damp girdle and wrinkled skirt.

Sometimes life was more than good at the Bain place. In the evenings we could listen to the radio; we had, luxury of luxuries! a thousand-hour battery for that radio. We could listen to Fibber McGee and Molly and the Jack Benny show in the evenings. And of course there was country western music during the day, and the news and stock market reports. There was an enormous pillow-shaped orange colored spider who made her home behind the radio in one of the window sills. I never bothered her.

Chapter 20

Pete's absences were becoming more frequent. And my first-born, my beautiful son Preston, was at the age of thirteen becoming my protector, my friend. Pete was beginning to be more and more unreliable, and I began to rely more and more on Preston and to look forward to the day when he would be fully grown and could assume the leadership of the family.

Esther had died of cancer and Percy had sold his ranch and moved to a place a few miles up the river from the Bain place. My heart was heavy for Percy. Esther had been his "rock of Gibralter," his constant love and support, even when he drank. Percy was a binge drinker, but he kept his sense of direction when he recovered each time whereas Pete seemed somehow to lose his focus.

"I just came down to see how you were getting along, Mom," Preston said one day, standing tall enough to be eye to eye with me.

He had been helping at Percy's ranch when he heard that Pete was drinking again. That was a sunny day in mid-June.

Preston died at dusk on the day after his thirteenth birthday that August. He and a young hired man of Percy's had ridden their horses out on the hillsides looking for a little bunch of missing heifers. Preston was riding Spade, our favorite and most dependable horse, a black gelding with a white mark on his forehead. As they approached the ranch, Spade stepped into a freshly dug gopher hole and flipped over on Preston, crushing his chest. Joe, the hired hand, in a panic gathered Preston in his arms and raced for the ranch house.

Laura, Pete's sister, was at the ranch with her children. She put Preston into her car and started for Dubois with him. There was a doctor resident in Dubois at the time, but Preston died on the way there. His ribs had penetrated his lungs and he bled to death. Laura later told Carol that she had felt the moment when he died.

Pete and I had been in Lander that day. Carol had spent the day at Burris with her cousin Sally. Carol and Sally had been riding horseback in the area, and we had waited for them at the Burris store on our way home. Carol said later that she had felt uneasy all day and eager to get home. Laura met us at the crossroad; it was full dark by then. We were on our way in to Percy's place, and she was coming back from Dubois. She stopped her car, and I heard her say, as if in a dream, "Allyene, I am so sorry."

Dear God, Preston has been dead for almost fifty years, and there is still that empty place in my heart. What will he be like when I see him in heaven, I wonder. Will he still be thirteen as he was when his horse fell and crushed him — piercing his lungs with his shattered ribs? Has he witnessed the lives we have all lived during the intervening years? It was consoling to think that Esther was there to greet him. It is consoling to think they will be there to greet me. For years I had thought little about my faith. On the ranch, we were far from any church, and we lived pretty much without a calendar or even a clock, to let us know what day it was or what time.

Jack came up to the ranch and took us to his home at Crowheart that night. He and his wife Mary Jane tended to our needs and those of Carol and Danny and Susie. Mary Jane fed the children and got them to bed. The Episcopal priest from Our Father's House at Ethete, a small community on the reservation fifty miles from Crowheart, arrived at Jack's house at six o'clock the next morning.

We were acquainted with this priest, "Coach" Wilson. He had waded the river to visit us on a few occasions, and had baptized our children in a little log church in town. I rode with Coach to Lander to make funeral arrangements. In shock I cried out to him, "Why did this have to happen to me?" Gently but firmly he replied, "Why not to you? What sets you apart from mothers all over the world who see their children die, whether from accident, or from disease or starvation?" I felt the justice of that. And I felt later, at Preston's funeral, the attitude of hope and peace with which Coach conducted the funeral.

Pete and I comforted one another as best we could in the days before and during the funeral. After the service we took Carol and Danny and Susie and went back to the Bain place. Shortly after we got home, Pete left and I did not see him again for ten days. His way of dealing with his grief was drinking with his friends. I had to find a way to deal with mine. During that time alone with the children I was numb. Fixing food and doing normal day to day chores, I worked in a daze.

One day as I fixed a meal, I set the table for four children. When the food was ready I called, "Preston and Carol Ann, Danny and Susie, come in and eat." When I realized what I had done, there was a frightening wave that threatened to overwhelm me. Suddenly I knew that there was no way out of realizing the truth, the finality, of my son's death. And there came a moment of stillness within me, and a Presence with me. A voice spoke into my heart and said to me, "This cup of pain is yours. You must drink it to the dregs." It enabled me at that moment to let the awful realization wash over me.

93

I could, with the help of the One who stood with me, let the knowledge come: I would never again in this life see my child, my first-born son, Preston. The son in whom I had begun to place my hopes for the future.

For several days after that I felt an inner peace. Even though Preston's bloody chaps hung in the entryway to remind me of his death, I was achingly aware of the beauty around me. Cottonwoods were brilliantly yellow that fall at the Bain place. Their juxtaposition against the deep and glowing blue of the September sky brought a kind of peace and even joy, as I grieved. It was as if I became two people for a time. There was a hollow me who had a permanent emptiness, and there was a me who stood alongside and saw the trees and the sky and the people moving around me.

Percy occupied a special place in my heart during that time; he had lost his mother and his wife within less than two years, and now this loss of his first grandchild was devastating to him. I hurt for him.

One day I encountered a neighbor in the drug store in town, and she asked, "How are Preston and Carol Ann?" I said, "You know, Preston died." Her face blanched. "Oh, dear God, I knew that. Oh, my God. Please forgive me." My heart expanded to encompass the horror she was feeling. It was hard to help her get past that simple mistake. Somehow, understanding her embarrassment helped me to begin coming together as a person again.

Chapter 21

After Pete came home from journeying through pain in his own way, I began to long for a different place to live. I wanted a place with people. I felt the need for the company of other women. I fantasized about doing community things; PTA, church work, square dances, school events.

When a small hay ranch at Burris became available, we got a government loan and bought it. We moved from the Bain place and into the community of Burris and Crowheart. We lived on that little place for five years. The move proved to be one of the biggest mistakes of my life.

While I had hoped for community in that place, what came about was confusion instead. Initially I found comfort in being a part of church life at a little log church at Crowheart. We had neighbors within walking distance. Pete and other cowboys roped calves in our large corral on Sunday afternoons, and the other wives and I visited while the children played. The homemakers' club afforded a monthly get-together. And I joined an artists' guild and undertook to learn oil painting. I loved all of that.

We were prevailed upon to take two small Arapaho boys into our home for a time. They had been found alone in their parents' home with an eight year old sister. The younger of the boys was still a bottle baby. His bottle was filled with sour milk when the children were discovered in the house, and all the food there was lay on the floor in the dirty kitchen; it consisted of a slab of bologna and an opened loaf of bread. We took the boys in. They were adorable. Unfortunately, I did not notice that Susie was having a big problem with having two younger children brought into her family.

Things grew to be enormously busy. Too busy! Jimmy Hill was a short, very dark Shoshone cowboy with a thick head of silvery white hair. He had a wisdom I greatly admired. He stopped at our place often, and I always enjoyed having him sit at my kitchen table, with his spurs and cowboy hat on, ready to ride on after eating whatever food I had prepared. He was at our house one day. He watched all the coming and going. In addition to Danny and Susie, and the little boys, I was caring for four neighbor children while their mother went to town. Other people kept dropping in. I was trying to get ready to go to a meeting. Pete and another cowboy rode in expecting a meal.

Jimmy observed all this for a bit. "Too many lines cross in this house," he commented in a matter of fact way. Too many, indeed!

While we lived in the isolation of the Bain place, Pete's alcoholism had been a hidden and ignorable part of our lives. In the Burris-Crowheart community, Pete and other men often stumbled in to our house in the middle of the night, drunk and cursing and quarreling, carrying guns and knives. The children would waken and come in to my bedroom, frightened. This began to happen more and more frequently.

Chapter 22

It was an icy, blustery day at the ranch at Burris when Pete stood in the kitchen, swaying a little, reeking of stale beer. His eyes were bloodshot. He had several day's growth of beard. His clothes stunk of spilled drinks and old sweat, as if he had not changed them for days. Pete had been drinking more and more since we had moved from the Bain place. He often came home only when he was too sick to drink any more. Each time, he would sleep off the effects of the alcohol, get cleaned up, and then leave again.

"How would you feel," he asked, slurring his words and grinning foolishly, "about raising a little black baby?" When I asked him what he meant, he turned away and would not say any more. He was not quite drunk, but not quite sober, either.

It was late November when he confronted me with that odd question. It made me more than uneasy. I was beginning to be desperate. He had drunk steadily since shipping the cattle in October. Our bills were not being paid, and our mortgage payment was due.

Pete was gone at Christmas. Christmas day that year was the coldest, bleakest day of my life. Our three children and two little Indian foster children we had taken, had food only because Percy had come down and brought us some groceries. Percy ate dinner with us, and cursed the behavior of his son. "Why don't you call the sheriff and have him arrested?" he grumbled, notwithstanding the fact that the nearest telephone was ten miles away at Crowheart, and I had no transportation.

Della, a neighbor whose husband also drank, stopped by our house one evening when Pete was gone. It had been about a month since he had asked that question, and a couple of weeks since Christmas. "Della, do you know what is going on with Pete?" I begged. She hesitated. "Well, I have heard that he might be staying down with a young woman at Fort Washakie part of the time." She mentioned a name. I knew of the family, but not the woman she mentioned. I asked some questions and learned that the woman, Maggie, was only a few years older than Carol Ann, and had the reputation of being wild and a heavy drinker.

A few days after my conversation with Della, Pete came home drunk again one night in late December. He was sleeping in a drunken stupor. I was furious. I went into the bedroom where he was snoring and violently shook him awake. "You bastard!" I screamed. "Where is your squaw lover? "I picked up a chair and hurled it against the wall. "Della told me what you've been up to, you filthy dog-eating son of a bitch!"

"Aw, honey," he said sheepishly, "I just got mixed up in something I didn't know how to get out of. I promise that I will straighten up. I just felt so guilty that I started drinking more. I'm glad you found out. I will never see her again. I promise I'll quit drinking and we can just forget the whole thing and get on with our life."

Placated, but in a daze of hurt and betrayal, I went on doing what needed to be done, taking care of the house and the children. I think that Pete may have tried to stay sober for a short time, but it didn't last. He said one morning, "I'm going over and help Jack move some cows. I'll be home by the middle of the afternoon." About the time I expected him home, I saw our pickup drive up the lane and bypass our drive. Thinking he might just have gone to Crowheart to get our mail, I waited. He didn't come home.

I waited up until midnight. With my heart pounding, I watched for car lights in the lane. Then I fell on my face on the cold linoleum of the kitchen floor and I wept, I screamed, I sobbed. Finally I began to pray. "God," I cried out, "what shall I do? Help me! Oh, God, you have to help me!

I visualized killing Pete and his woman. I fantasized killing myself, lying dead before him and watching him cry in sorrow for what he had done to me. But then I saw my children. And I knew in my heart that I had to get away from that place before I did something that could not be undone, something that would inflict irreparable damage on people who loved us.

Although she was reluctant to do so, I prevailed upon Della to take the children and me down to Fort Washakie, to a bar where I knew Pete sometimes drank. He was there, leaning on the bar. I told him I was leaving and taking the children. He had been drinking but wasn't entirely drunk. He followed me from the bar and out to the car.

Pete grinned at me and said casually, "You just go on back home, and I'll be there in the morning." A burst of rage exploded in my brain. I slapped him with all my strength and left him standing there. Della drove the children and me into Lander, and we stayed with Jack and Mary Jane, who were in town on business. Our foster children were taken by Della and her family until they could be placed elsewhere, and my heart ached at leaving them. The next morning, Jack loaned me a hundred dollars for bus fare, and I took Danny and

Susie to Laramie. Carol had married a young man on the reservation a few months before, and would stay there.

Chapter 23

A young vicar, Howie, who had served the little mission at Crowheart had become a friend during the five years we lived in the community. He had since moved to Laramie as archdeacon in the Episcopal diocese. My first inclination was to find some help and guidance by talking to him. Filled with self-pity, I poured out my sad story to him, wiping my tears and blowing my nose. He listened quietly, and then stepped right over all my emotional outpourings and said calmly, "Well, I see two things you will have to do first off. You will need a place to live, and you will have to find a job to support your children." Wisely, he had managed immediately to pull me out of the past and turn my face to the future.

Housing would not be a problem. Viola and Jess, my good friends from the war years, owned some apartment buildings in Laramie. They happened right then to have an apartment available for us to move into right away. My children had never lived in such close quarters. They were accustomed to the freedom of the ranch. However, it was far from my mind to consider their feelings. I was much too involved in my own problems and emotional turmoil to be much aware of their needs.

With the help of my clergy friend, Howie, I found work at the Episcopal cathedral in Laramie. The dean of the cathedral was looking for a person who would be free and willing to train for religious education and youth work in that church. After an interview with the dean, I committed to take three months of intensive training in Ohio, and then come back as parish assistant at the cathedral. I began working in the church office in February. The training program began in June.

On June ninth, I checked in at the program and began what would be a crash course in religious education. It was excellent training. At the end of three months of hard work with a group of sixteen trainees and various faculty and visiting clergy, I was ready, intellectually, to do whatever would be needed at the cathedral in the field of Christian education. I had learned a smattering of theology, some basic training in age-level characteristics of children and young people, some sensitivity-training skills, techniques for leading adult Bible study, and a thorough familiarity with the church school curriculum materials then in use at the church where I would work.

There had been some solid teaching on the Bible, and on church history. We had lived three months together, sharing meals and working together for as many as sixteen hours a day. We had shared our life stories, and many of us had become close friends. The program ended on the thirty-first day of August.

Carol and her husband were expecting a baby in late August. The group and our leaders in the program had been looking forward to celebrating the arrival of my first grandchild. He didn't make his appearance until the day after I returned home. On the first day of September my first grandchild was born.

I worked at the cathedral for seven years. Someone had told me, "After seven years, you will have done everything that you are going to do, and you will be looking for a move." It was true. By the beginning of the seventh year there, I found that I was simply beginning to repeat what I had done before, and less effectively. I wrote a friend in Ohio that I really felt that I was ready for a change.

Chapter 24

My heart aches with regret that I had not, during those seven years, truly seen my youngest daughter, Susie. She had begun to act out almost from the day we moved from the reservation. I failed to see the pattern. Susie had been a troubled child from the time she started to school. I came to see, much later, that she needed — and her father and I needed — professional help. Pete and I had been too self-centered, too wrapped up in our own private miseries, to respond to that need, even had such help been available in our community.

Susie had begun to stay out all night; she was thirteen years old and had begun drinking and smoking marijuana with a group of other young teens. Hoping to help Susie, Carol and her husband had taken her to live with them, hoping that a more structured home life might give her something she needed. It hadn't worked out.

Danny had gone back to Lander to stay for a summer with his uncle Jack. While I was alone, all my children elsewhere, I met and became involved with a young foreign student at the university, there to complete his education. He made me feel like a new woman. "You are so sharp! You are beautiful!" he told me. And I felt sharp and beautiful for the first time in my life. It was like salve to my wounded ego. After two years of waiting, I had divorced Pete. I had done a little dating, but had found no one who had attracted me. In this new relationship I found healing, even though I knew that it would not be permanent. We went out dancing and drinking with his friends in the local lounges, and within a few months, he moved in with me.

Then Susie returned home and life became a nightmare. One crisis after another ensued, and she finally was arrested and taken to jail for having in her possession a radio which she said she had stolen from a local shop. After a hearing in juvenile court, I was given a choice in Susie's behalf; either she would spend time in the state mental hospital where there was supposedly a juvenile alcoholics rehabilitation program, or she would be sent to the state reformatory for girls. My thinking was that the better of the options would be the mental health facility.

"You have to get this guy out of your house," I was informed. "And you need to seek psychological counseling." I complied with both recommendations. All the time that he had lived with me, a part of me had known that what we were doing was wrong, especially because of what I represented in my career. Yet, I had been able to rationalize it, to separate my personal life from what I was doing in the church. Some of the church's teaching was helping me to do that. Participation in the "situational ethics" teaching which was popular at the time, and studying books that maintained that there are no absolutes and that "God is dead" made it easy to avoid thinking about the teaching I had been given as a young Baptist about right and wrong conduct.

We were into the sixties, and the concensus was, "If it feels good, do it." However, I could not excuse my behavior on those grounds. Certainly I had had a thorough grounding in Christian morality. I knew in my deepest heart that I was living a lie, but I simply had ignored my conscience in the same way that I had put my responsibility for my children to the back of my mind. I was a religious person and a Christian education worker, but I was far from realizing what it meant to be a Christian.

Chapter 25

It was with the sense of beginning a new life that I accepted a position at the church in Ohio. Danny and I gathered together our few belongings and took a Greyhound bus to Cleveland. Danny would finish his last year of high school and I would be working in a suburban church that had a program that would challenge every bit of my ability and learning.

I had never learned to drive in all the years on the ranch or in Laramie. It was imperative that I learn to drive and get a car within a few weeks after I arrived for the new position. We had found an apartment in a building owned by the choir director at the church. It was in a neighboring community and fifteen miles from the church.

Our first friend in the new community was our landlord. He had picked us up in Cleveland and taken us to the church, and then to the apartment where we would live. He was incredibly kind. We found out that he was a banker, and he and his mother owned the building in which our apartment was. His mother lived in the same building and she graciously welcomed Danny and me.

Richard directed both the youth and adult choirs, and was a member of the governing body of the church. In the course of our particular church duties, he and I were frequently brought together. He was solicitous, capable and self-assured, and I grew to admire him tremendously. He often inquired how Danny was getting along in school, and whether we were comfortable in the apartment.

We learned that Richard lived near the church with his wife and three young daughters. Now and again he appeared at the church with his youngest daughter, who was about five years old. Richard seemed to spend a good amount of his free time caring for his daughters, particularly the youngest and some of her friends. I was impressed. "What a wonderful loving father he is," I thought.

Shortly after Dan and I moved into our apartment, Susie was released from the hospital. She was eighteen years old. She wanted to become a beautician, and I was able to get her enrolled in beauty school, and she tried to learn but found that she did not have enough education to handle it. I was working long hours at the church, and she was too much alone. Crisis after crisis developed, and each was solved with the help of some friends in the church.

Danny got enrolled in school. His worst nightmares had to do with my learning to drive. I frequently got lost in the area, sometimes in heavy three-lane traffic. Changing lanes was a terrible challenge. Drivers behind me would lay on their horns. Sometimes my knees would jerk with tension as I tried to maintain my self-control. "God, Mom," Danny would moan, covering his eyes and hunching down in the passenger seat of my little yellow Ford Comet. It was a very real prayer that he said.

About a year after I began work in that church, Richard elected to join an evening encounter group of which I was co-leader with one of the diocesan Christian education staff. For the first time since I had met him, Richard seemed somewhat unsure of himself. I sensed that he was troubled, but he shared nothing of that nature with the group. Rather, he tended to be a helpful and reassuring presence with others as they shared their concerns.

One day at the church I mentioned that I had some business in the city. Richard suggested that I stop at the bank. He would take me to lunch and discuss with me some questions I had about the preparation of my income tax. During the course of our conversation at lunch, he asked me about my life, what had brought me to Ohio, and what had happened with my marriage. I shared something of my story, and described some of the painful incidents that led to my divorce and eventually to my career in Christian education.

To my surprise, Richard's eyes filled with tears. "How could you deal with it, having your whole life collapse around you?" he asked. I wondered at the emotion in his voice. He said little more at the time. As time went on, in some conversations with Myrtle, Richard's mother, there were indications that there was less than complete harmony in Richard's home. Mostly I attributed this to Myrtle's seeming jealousy of Richard's wife and his mother-in-law.

One day in my office at the church, Richard seemed particularly sad. He told me that he and his wife had been seeking counsel with the rector. "She has said that I am incapable of satisfying a woman sexually," he said. "Are you afraid that is true?" I asked. He didn't respond. He did go on to tell me that his wife had asked him for a divorce some eight years earlier. She had been and continued to be, he told me, involved with another man.

"He was one of our neighbors," Richard said, "and we all used to gather at a swimming pool and have parties." Later he confessed that he hated those gatherings and felt ridiculed. In an effort to save his marriage, he told me, he had bought a home in another area and moved his family. He had hoped against hope that this would solve the problem, but it had not done so. Richard had learned from several sources that the affair was continuing, and he was contemplating getting a divorce. He hated the idea. It would break up his home and deprive his daughters of a normal family life. My feeling at that revelation was sadness that such a caring and responsible man should be so bereft and bewildered.

Chapter 26

With my work at the church, and my home in the apartment owned by Richard and Myrtle, Richard and I were continually being brought together. Dan and Richard had become good friends. I began to think enviously of the life Richard's wife seemed eager to throw away. Sometimes I imagined how it would be to eat at the dinner table with him in a home that we shared. Dangerous imaginings.

One evening after a particularly emotional encounter group session, Richard was driving me home. He was sharing with me some of the fun things he and his youngest daughter had done during the week before. Impulsively, I reached over and took his hand. I said, "You are a great example of a real family man."

"I wish other people thought so," he replied gruffly. "Things are going from bad to worse. My wife is still seeing this guy." I knew that this was so, but I could not tell him that I did. Myrtle had been spying on Richard's wife for some time and she could not keep her findings to herself. She told Dan and me that she had driven by the apartment of the man involved, and had seen Richard's wife's car parked in the driveway. The whole situation seemed like a mess to me, and I thought Richard was misguided and foolish to stay in such a predicament.

Dan had enrolled at Cleveland State University, and had completed two semesters. At enrollment time for the third semester, he was unable to get the classes he needed, and did not get signed up for enough hours to qualify him as a full time student. Within weeks, he received that "Greetings from the President" letter, advising him that he was to appear for induction into the United States Army. He left, and after six months training and one furlough, was shipped out to Viet Nam.

Richard seemed to be living his life out of a series of boxes. There appeared to be little consistency or continuity in his life because of an apparent inability for him to set a direction for his life. At work, he was Richard the banker. At church he was Richard the choir director and church leader. When he was at home he was, by his own admission, both mother and father to his three daughters. But who, indeed, I wondered, was Richard the person? And eventually I asked him just that question. "Who are you, really? What do you want out of life? Where do you want to be in ten years? Twenty years?"

After all these years I know and confess that I had already begun to know deep down what I wanted and where I wanted to be. I wanted him, and I wanted to spend the rest of my life with him. Certainly I could not have said that to him, nor even to myself — but there was a design and a direction to those questions — and I am sure that I sensed that they could lead into a different kind of relationship with him. It did. After about another year of friendship, we fell into an affair. It seemed at the time as if it had just happened, as if it were unplanned and unexpected by either of us. It was not a happy situation for either of us.

Richard and his wife eventually worked out a divorce settlement and proceedings were begun. While the divorce was taking place, I left my position at the church and went to a small town in Utah where Carol was living with her husband and children. It was uncertain how things were going to work out. The rector at our church had been as sympathetic to us as he could be. He had tried to counsel the two people and was aware of the inner workings of that marriage, which he conceded had been no marriage at all.

During the time I was out west with Carol and her family, Richard's divorce was finalized. One day a few weeks later, the

117

telephone rang, and it was Richard calling, "You have to come back here right away," he told me, with excitement in his voice. "We can adopt a baby, but we have to get married first," he said. I was astounded. "What are you talking about?" I could make no sense of the conversation. "Are you all right?" I had to wonder if Richard's mind had snapped.

"What? I feel great!" was his response. "There is a girl in the hospital here. She is going to deliver in a week or so, and she wants to give her baby up for adoption. But she wants to know the adoptive parents." This still made no sense to me.

Richard explained. Dan, who had done a year in Viet Nam, had subsequently returned home. He had been dating a young divorcee with two infant daughters. This young woman had advertised for a live-in nanny for her children, and she had received a response from a girl who had become pregnant. The girl had not wanted her parents nor her fiance, who was in Viet Nam, to learn of the pregnancy. Danny met the girl and was sympathetic.

"You and Mom like kids," Dan had suggested to Richard. "You should talk with Cindy and maybe adopt her baby. If you would take care of her hospital bills, I think she would be willing to let you have the baby." Richard had visited the girl, and she had assented to the plan, contingent upon her approval of me as the prospective mother.

118

Richard had approached the judge at the probate court, who had told him, "I don't even want to talk to you, unless and until you are married."

Confused and wondering, I flew back to Ohio. Richard had already rented a large, comfortable old home some thirty miles away from where Danny and I had lived. It was a restored historic large brick house on several acres, with a barn for Richard's daughters' horses and Shetland ponies. It was a lovely home which had been completely furnished and equipped by Richard and his girls, with the help of an interior decorator.

Feeling strange and disoriented, I moved in with them. Richard and I had a hasty, simple wedding in the village church. Cindy visited with us. She was a sensible and pleasant young woman, and I liked her immediately. After a few days, she consented freely to our adoption of her child.

Shortly after, Richard and I met with the judge and the referee at the probate court. It was a short meeting. The judge said to Richard that he would like twenty minutes or so to speak with me alone in another room of the courthouse. He meant to get some feeling about what sort of mother I would be.

When we were seated in the office, the judge leaned back in his chair and spoke, not unkindly. "How do you think you will handle all the work and fuss of raising an infant at your age?" he queried. "You are well over forty. You have been doing other kinds of things unlike maintaining a home and raising small children, for quite a while. How do you think it will be, going back to formulas and diapers and all that?"

"Your Honor," I responded, "when I raised my children it was on a ranch where I carried water in two five gallon buckets a quarter of a mile from the river for washing and everything else. I had a wood stove and usually I had to gather and cut wood to heat the water. I did all the washing by hand or with an old gasoline washing machine. For most of the years there was no electricity or indoor plumbing. I think with all the modern conveniences we have in the house, I will have no problem taking care of a baby."

The judge and I were back with Richard in fewer than ten minutes. "I think she'll be fine," the judge smiled. We left the courthouse and went back home to prepare for the Christmas celebrations with Richard's daughters and my son Dan. We had been married just since Thanksgiving, and were just beginning to adjust to our new life together.

On the day after Christmas, we picked up our baby son from off a desk top in a basement room at the courthouse. It was a thrill, holding a little bundle of squirming, two-month old infant in my arms. It seemed entirely natural. And a new life was certainly beginning for our infant son, as well as for the rest of this newly combined family.

Chapter 27

Holding our warm, soft baby in our arms and caring for his simple needs was easy. We named the baby after Richard, and called him Ricky. He was an easy baby, happy and responsive most of the time. Richard and I both loved taking care of him. Even Richard's girls seemed to enjoy having an infant in the house. Richard's three daughters were with their mother during the week and came to us for weekends, holidays and vacations.

In the process of trying to live up to the demands of this new life, I began to develop migraine headaches, often two a week. My thinking became confused. Richard loved having the girls with us, and did everything he could to keep them entertained and happy during the times they were in our care. Jealousy began to infiltrate my mind and heart, though I tried to hide it. I was an outsider in our household, I thought. Richard and the girls seemed to me to form a circle that kept me out. Between the headaches I was having and the medications the doctor prescribed to control the pain, I was spending days in a darkened bedroom with the covers over my head, immersed in misery.

Our family doctor began to be concerned for my health and sent me to the hospital for some tests, to ascertain whether there was some organic cause for the migraines. Nothing showed up in the tests. Finally one day the doctor sat on the side of the hospital bed and asked, "What is going on in your life right now?"

Suddenly there came a flash of understanding; of things I had not dealt with. Tears began to run down my face, and there was a vast easing of tension in my body. Because of the way I wanted people to see me I had resisted the need to face my real feelings and to express the anger that threatened to overwhelm my personality, and with it, my character. Self-pity was crippling my relationships. Later I came to realize that I had opened the door to jealousy and corrosive self-involvement and emotional upheaval.

At one time before Richard and I were married, I had sought reassurance about the future by consulting a ouija board, reading my horoscope, and consulting cards to tell the future. Such activities, I have since learned, are open doorways to darkness and evil spirits.

In the light of the training I had experienced in my career as a religious educator, it seems odd that I had so little understanding of the stress-producing factors in life, and so little ability to apply what I had learned, to my own life. Everything Richard and I had done as a couple had been almost tailor-made to fill our lives with tension and stress. For him, however, there was a refuge in his busy life as a banker, and in his dedication to keeping his daughters happy. This all served, I think, to keep him more or less insulated from some of the factors that affected my mental and emotional health.

Some of the factors in our marriage had to do with my own children and their place in this new family constellation. Dan had come back from Viet Nam with his own set of problems. We had not yet heard of "post-traumatic stress syndrome," but there had been many signs that he had been affected by his experience as a soldier, both during and after his time in the service.

Dan had won the Bronze Star with V for Valor medal, and yet his church and some of the citizens of his country treated him and other young heroes as pariahs. This was hurtful to him, particularly the attitude of the Episcopal church to which he had been dedicated. I was also hurt, not only by the church, but because I felt that Richard had little understanding of Dan's emotional state in that situation. I resented what I felt to be the off-hand treatment he gave to Dan's needs.

Carol and her husband and children moved to a nearby village. They bought a house and began to remodel it. Her presence in the area helped me to maintain a little equilibrium during those days of adjustment for Richard and me. She listened to my fancied grievances and took no sides. It helped to have a quiet listener. Talking to her helped me to sort out some of the confusion and inconsistencies in my thinking and emotions.

Susie was in and out of the family life during those first years; her behavior added to the confusion. She drank heavily. She took the family car one night and had an accident while drunk. A woman was injured, and Richard was angry about the complication to his insurance because of the accident. I was both angry and defensive. The frustration I felt was damaging to my relationship with Richard.

My envy and jealousy of Richard's daughters was aggravated by the complications of guilt and helplessness in my relationships with my children and my past mistakes. The thing was, I loved Richard's daughters at the same time I was jealous of them. My emotions were a mess. I had convinced myself that I was unappreciated and unloved and emotionally deprived.

The presence of the baby Ricky in our home, though sometimes physically exhausting as he grew bigger, brought what Dan called

125

"instant sanity" to our family life. Cuddling his warm body was comfort in the midst of confusion. Ricky's infant needs were simple and easily met, unlike the unspoken and too often unrecognized needs of the rest of this entangled household.

Chapter 28

The simple question asked by that wise doctor was the first step toward mental health for me. I was able at last to drop, at least in my thinking, the facade of sweetness and light in my attitude toward the girls, and face with a modicum of honesty the ugly feelings I had tried to conceal, even from myself.

Yes, I was furious with Richard, I could admit, because he was afraid of alienating his daughters by being the disciplinary parent when they were with us. I was angry and hurt when I seemed to be outside the circle of their life together. It seemed to me, however mistakenly, that Richard's primary motivation in life was to keep his children happy and entertained, and that he considered me the world's worst wet blanket.

Resentment toward the priority Richard placed on his relationship with his children dominated my thinking. I resented, too, what I imagined to be his irritation at the confusion brought into his life by mixing our families. I felt he was oblivious to my needs and the growing unhappiness I felt. If he loved me as he claimed, he should instinctively know how I felt. He finally put an end to that kind of thinking on my part.

"Damn it, Allyene," Richard exclaimed in total exasperation, at the end of one particularly confusing argument, "I want to give you anything and everything you need, but I will not play these guessing games with you. Tell me what you want! I will do everything I possibly can to see that you have it. But you will have to first figure out what it is and tell me. We're getting nowhere this way."

That was a word of wisdom I could recognize. It was a moment of God's grace in which I was brought to see my error. I saw the injustice of expecting the impossible of Richard, of demanding that he sort out the confused expectations I had, when I could not, myself, define what they were.

This was the first inkling I had that he also had a real need of my understanding as we worked to put this family together. Richard was honest with me, and I resolved in my heart that I would try to be more honest with him, and would speak more openly about my needs and feelings. Richard had, in that simple statement, taught me an important truth about myself and about our marriage.

Chapter 29

I turned fifty, and Ricky turned into a two year old. About that time, we bought an old house on forty-five acres of land and remodeled it. While we worked to clear the acreage and enlarge the house, Ricky was an exceedingly active and imaginative little bundle of energy.

One day, while he was supposed to be napping, he filled the steam radiators in two rooms, and also his little tennis shoes, with Crisco, and he painted the cat and a part of our newly painted ochre house · Williamsburg blue with paint meant for the dining room. He climbed to the second story of the house on a ladder left by the roofer. He went to sleep in a dark corner of the living room under a built-in bench alongside the fireplace. The police and I and several neighbors searched for him until he was finally discovered, curled up in that corner with one of our cats.

Where was I, that he could have all these adventures? There was a lot going on, claiming my attention! Richard had bought a baby chimpanzee for his youngest daughter. We called him Rusty. It was like having two two-year olds in the house. Except that one could climb walls and swing from the chandeliers. In many ways, the two of them were fun for the whole family, but at the same time they caused a lot of confusion.

Richard had a tennis court built. The girls and their friends came out on weekends and holidays and had tennis games with Richard. It was a rare weekend when there were not twenty or more young people on hand. Every holiday and birthday was an occasion for a family get-together and a special dinner. Cooking was a thing I enjoyed, and the gatherings were special.

We had pigs and steers, horses and Shetland ponies and a sheep that had to be sheared once a year. We had Bowser, Richard's dog who was growing old. Then Richard decided to raise some chickens. He bought some Auricanas, Polish chickens. They had feathery topknots that looked like umbrellas on their heads, and the hens laid eggs in several shades of green, from a light pastel to a deep olive. Richard often went off to town with cartons of green eggs for people who worked with him at the bank.

One morning in the chicken era, the phone rang an hour after Richard had ostensibly left for work at the bank. It was Binnie, Richard's secretary. "Where **is** he?" she asked. "Why, he left an hour ago," I answered. But, puzzled, I went to the window and looked out. There in the driveway sat the bank's green Cadillac convertible. Fearing that a heart attack or worse had hit Richard, I went outside. Very faintly, a voice was calling my name. When I followed the sound, it seemed to be coming from the chicken house. It was. I opened the chicken house door, and there was Richard — "all eggy and featherful" — his suit covered with feathers and chicken manure. The door had blown shut and latched on the outside, and he had tried, on his hands and knees, to crawl through the little square hole that the hens used to get into the chicken yard. Richard was extemely cross while I laughed hysterically. He was still snuffy as he called his office and then left to spend what was left of the day recovering his equilibrium and self-image at the bank.

We had a gander who stayed near the pond in our yard, and eyed me aggressively as I walked to the mailbox. Once he managed to intercept me at our back door, which unfortunately opened outward rather than inward. Before I could get into the house, he had flailed me with his wings, and bitten a baseball-sized blood blister on my thigh. I hated him. He fell in love with a snowmobile in our yard, and guarded it fiercely. Nearly everyone in the family felt his animosity at one time or another.

131

Richard loved to garden. He planted tomatoes and squash, green beans and peas.

Everything grew; we had beautiful vegetables. That is, we had **tons** of peas and beans and zucchini and tomatoes. We froze them, gave them away, and still they came. Through the summer I waited patiently for one canteloup to ripen. One morning I went out to the garden to check on the melon, and found an empty rind. Some little critter had eaten all the insides.

Our home was large and comfortable. I had help with Ricky and with the cleaning. One day a week, I was free to do anything I wanted, with Mrs. Mitchell there to clean and watch Ricky and Rusty the Chimp. It was the situation I had dreamed of; Richard and I at our dinner table in a home we shared. Perfect.

There was still a smouldering resentment in me, though. Even when I enjoyed preparing meals, I felt put-upon and unappreciated in the midst of all the activity. I had the younger children under foot while the older teenagers and Richard played. For some time I kept Richard's first grandchild, a little girl Ricky's age, while her mother went on with her education. It was something I offered to do, and I loved the little girl, but continued to have mixed-up feelings about practically everything in our life. And Richard was pragmatic and unimaginative.

The migraines were gone, but my thoughts and emotions were still confused and disturbing. We seemed to have no center from which to live. We had, of course, both been religious people, and soon after our marriage, had found a little Episcopal mission that attracted us. The vicar was a young priest whom I had come to know from various leadership training events and youth conferences in the diocese while I worked in religious education. Richard and I decided to join that parish and to become active in it. Actually, Richard became active. I went to Sunday services with him.

We went to church Sunday after Sunday, angry and either quarreling or coldly ignoring one another. Putting on our Sunday faces, we got through the worship service, socialized separately at the coffee hour, and then took up our anger again on the way home. Richard was outgoing and well-liked. I was filled with envy at the ease with which he was able to drop his irritation and relate to young and old, with men, women and children in the congregation. I felt awkward and ill at ease, knowing how far short I was falling in my duty as wife and as mother to the assortment of family we had brought together.

Richard and I had sought counseling from the priest in our struggles to become a real family. Charles, the priest, had given us his best counsel, and his friendship as well. Still, there was only so much that friendship and wise counsel could do for a marriage that was floundering. Richard and I had both become filled with self-pity as a result of our unfulfilled expectations of one another and our life together. Each of us was trying desperately to get the other to hear and understand the aching void inside.

Being married to a successful, attractive and financially well off banker, I was out of my depth socially. The art of casual conversation was one I had never learned. I had no idea how to dress for the social occasions his position required. And having achieved no real identity of my own, I was unequal to the challenge of presenting myself as a person in the midst of a gathering of seemingly self-confident men and women.

Charles, our priest, had studied psychology and was a good counselor, but it was not enough to help us. He was sensitive and caring. Once, in a session at our house, I swallowed hard when Richard said something critical of me. Charles glanced at me and said, "Isn't it interesting how often we try to swallow our hurt?"

Chapter 30

Something happened in that little mission church and to Charles, in our second year of attendance there. Charles was prayed with by a young couple who had led some youth meetings in the area. One of Charles' daughters had attended one of the meetings. She reported to her parents that there had been some teachings and evangelistic prayers there. Charles and his wife thought that the implications of that were questionable. Charles set up a meeting with the young leaders of those meetings.

"I had a real picture in my mind of what they would look like," Charles reported later. "She would be frumpy, with thick glasses and wrinkled stockings, and her mousy hair would be in a bun. He would wear baggy pants and his hair would be shaggy. His shoes would be dusty, and his coat-sleeves too short."

They appeared at his office, and Charles was taken by surprise. The man was about thirty-five, tall, handsome and self-assured. His wife was extremely attractive, well-dressed and friendly. Both had what Charles could only describe as "a glow" about them. They talked for some time. They spoke with Charles about something he had heard little of, in his training and experience as a clergyman. They described the power of the Holy Spirit.

"Can we pray with you for the infilling of the Holy Spirit?" they asked. He assented, with little confidence in the idea but a real wish to hear more and to find out more about this unusual couple. They prayed with him, and then after a little more conversation, they left.

"It felt strange," Charles told us later. "No one had **ever** offered to pray with me before." He had felt nothing different as they had prayed, but then, he said later, "I felt compelled to go into the church and kneel before the altar." On his knees in the church, he described to us later, "I asked God, 'if what they said to me is real, I want to know it. Show me what that is,' I prayed."

Suddenly Charles found his face wet with tears, and a strange and wonderful language poured forth from his mouth. Charles had been "filled with the Holy Spirit." Neither he nor, later, any of us had any notion of what that would mean. We would soon learn.

Up to this time, our church had attracted some thirty to forty · people who sat as far as possible apart from one another during Sunday services, and found it difficult, and for some even distasteful to "pass the peace," that is, to extend the hand of fellowship within the church service. Our fellowship was social and had nothing much to do with our religion. We were somewhat more like a social club which incidentally had a worship service.

As the Spirit began to move in Charles' life and then to extend into the whole church, incredible things began to happen. A wind of love began to sweep through the congregation. At first a gentle breeze, it became a mighty gale. It changed us. Lives were turned around, and people began to minister to one another. Our church grew. People began to come from communities miles away, irresistably drawn by the love that evidenced itself in the life of the congregation. And some of the great people of God came to teach us. Roman Catholic nuns came and taught us how to praise God in song. Men and women of different denominations who were mature in the Spirit came to give teachings that would help us to grow.

Chapter 31

Needless to say, both Richard and I were eventually touched by that Spirit. It was from that touch that we came to the place of praying a prayer that would bring a series of events into our lives with the force of a tornado. It would change us forever.

Late one night, I lay in bed, quietly furious. Richard had come home a few minutes earlier, and had come to bed. He had turned on his side away from me, and had said nothing. We lay back to back for what seemed to be forever. Finally I could contain my anger no longer, and I asked him, "Why do you bother to come home at all?" My voice was shaking with pent-up indignation and rage.

For many weeks it seemed that Ricky and I had scarcely seen Richard, except in the hours when the girls and their friends were at home. He breakfasted with clients, lunched with clients, and then had dinner meetings with clients. He had become president of the fastest growing bank in the western United States, and even many of his hours at home on weekends were spent either on the telephone or entertaining clients or the bank's lawyers at our home.

I had heard many of the conversations that took place then, and I had an uncomfortable feeling that this business was moving too far, too fast. At times I had a clear vision of a house of cards disintegrating and blowing away in a strong wind. Ignorant as I was of the banking business, still I kept hearing words my Dad had often said to me. "Take a little time and use a little foresight, Sis!" It seemed to me that in the excitement of the bank's growth, Richard and his associates were barely pausing to think.

"You know, I am sick to death of your whining and complaining," Richard snapped at me that night. He jerked impatiently and moved further to his side of the bed. "You liked what you saw when I married you. I never heard you complain that I was a busy banker then!"

"You were never too busy to spend time with me then, either," I reminded him.

"Well, why would I want to spend time with you, the way you are bitching and whining all the time now?" was his response. I was silenced for a time. In my heart I felt that I had a legitimate complaint. On the kitchen calendar I had marked for a few weeks the hours Richard had spent at home each day and evening. They were few, and I knew it was unreasonable to hope to maintain a marriage that way.

"We have been learning at church that the husband is supposed to be the spiritual leader of the family." I finally in despair spoke into the dark. "You are leading this family nowhere. Your ambition is destroying us as a family."

I lay there tense, expecting an explosion. Moments went by. Then Richard said quietly, "Maybe we had better pray about this." A few more moments passed, and then he spoke again. "Lord," he prayed, "if we are not living our lives the way You want us to, please take them over and bring us back into Your way."

This prayer had more power than we could have dreamed. It brought about a set of circumstances and changed our lives in ways we never would have expected nor wanted. Before we knew it, we were in the grip of something that felt like a hurricane, and we were confused and terrified.

"Lord, what **is** this?" we cried. "What are you doing to us?" And yet, what we would learn would be that there can be peace in the middle of chaos; the chaos we would face in the weeks and months that followed the prayer that Richard prayed that night.

Chapter 32

Some weeks after that prayer, word came that Mom had suffered a stroke. I flew home to be with her and to try to help Dad. While I was there, Richard called to say that something shocking had occurred, and that the bank had closed. As soon as Mom's condition was stabilized and she was out of the hospital, I returned home. When I arrived there, I was horrified to learn that Richard had been accused by the government of fraudulant banking practices. He was astounded. He was certain that he had broken no laws.

The investigation that ensued went on for months, and eventually Richard was indicted. He elected to fight the charges, and one government attorney informed him, "Admit a few little charges and we will be easy on you. Fight us, and we will nail your hide to the wall." Richard hired an attorney.

An interesting situation developed. One of the board of directors of the bank was approached by an FBI agent. This man had a son who was being tried on some drug charges. He told Richard and his attorney that the agent had offered him a deal in behalf of the son. "Give us something on Richard and we'll let the charges against your son be lessened." The man refused to compromise his principles. There were others who had no such integrity, however.

Richard lost no sleep during the months of the trial. He and I experienced continual peace throughout the whole process. Our church surrounded us with love. Nevertheless, just before Christmas, Richard was convicted of three counts of fraud. Sentencing would take place immediately following the holidays. We celebrated Christmas and New Year's Eve in the company of the assembled congregation of our church.

During the time of the trial and while we waited for the sentence to come down, my concern was chiefly for Myrtle, Richard's mother, and for his daughters and Ricky. In the midst of the confusion I found a transformed faith and strength. And Richard found in himself an unaccustomed patience and humility that enabled him to triumph over his circumstances.

In the interim between the bank's closing and the beginning of the court proceedings, one of the bank's directors approached Richard with a suggestion. Since we would need an income, he offered to sell Richard his share in a heavy equipment dealership, and would take a share of the company's profits in lieu of a down payment.

We had run out of money for household expenses. Richard had stood in line at the unemployment office, but there was no help immediately available. We prayed for a solution for the emergency need to meet current bills and to buy food. Richard had at one time gone to Saudi Arabia on bank business, and before he left, he had put cash for expenses into a box on a shelf in the closet.

As we prayed about our urgent need, suddenly I saw in my mind's eye that box in the closet, and went to look. In the box was two hundred dollars in cash, exactly enough to take care of the needs of the moment. It seemed like a sign that God had been taking care of us.

The judge pronounced sentence shortly after the beginning of the new year. Everyone in the courtroom gasped. Three four-year sentences; which would run consecutively, not concurrently! Twelve years! Even the attorneys for the government looked surprised.

Having won their case, the lawyers for the government concurred with Richard's request for time to settle some affairs and then present himself to Allenwood prison camp in Pennsylvania by the end of

June. Just before Richard turned himself in at Allenwood, one of the men from our church drove into our yard and told Richard excitedly, "I just had a vision and I have to tell you about it," he cried. "I saw you sitting at a desk writing and looking excited and happy," he went on. "I don't know what it meant, but I know it was a vision, and I know that it was for you!"

Chapter 33

It is hard now to believe that we were so yielded and so at peace with the circumstances we were in at the time. After a short period, Richard was allowed visitors. Almost every week there were friends from the church who wanted to take me and some of the family members to spend a few hours at the prison.

People joke about the government prison at Allenwood, as if it were some sort of resort. It is not. It is prison. As a visitor you are required to give up your purse or other items to be searched. Prisoners may be, and sometimes are, subjected to humiliating treatment. One man who had requested that his wife bring him a Roman Catholic missal, was strip-searched and transported to a maximum security prison nearby while authorities investigated the "missile" his wife had listed among the things she was carrying. (Their spelling, not hers!)

One day when he called home, Richard was forced to hang up suddenly in the middle of a conversation with me. He was being threatened by another prisoner, a convicted murderer who had served most of his sentence elsewhere and was at Allenwood waiting for his release. This man wanted to use the telephone and wouldn't wait. It was a frightening experience.

We certainly had an opportunity to understand the wisdom of living one day at a time. We learned to trust God for our future. One Thanksgiving passed. Ricky and Pam, Richard's youngest daughter, and I were able to visit at Christmas and actually sit at a table and eat with Richard on Christmas Day. Normally our visiting hours were spent sitting side by side in straight chairs, in an area not unlike a bus station.

On Thanksgiving Day, I was alone and took a cab to Allenwood from the motel where I was staying. The driver was an elderly man. I asked him what he was doing for Thanksgiving besides working. He told me, "I made a rocking horse for our grandson, and my wife is taking it to him in the town where our son lives, about a hundred miles from here. I wanted to go, but I needed to work. She offered to stay but, well — hell; I told her to go and have a good time, and bring me back some pictures." It was raining, the windshield wipers were rhythmic, and it was a moment of shared sadness.

Richard and I learned to be thankful for small blessings. We also learned that we could make friends in that situation and care about others who were there. We were blessed with kind taxi drivers and friendly waitresses at the nearby restaurants. We were sustained by the unfailing love of our friends at home, at church and in our community.

In retrospect, those days and weeks and months seem to have passed quickly and with a lot of sameness. I worked at the equipment company and drew a small salary. We simply marked time, certain that God had a plan for us and that He would disclose it in His own time. In the meantime we would just carry on as best we could, while hoping for a miracle.

In the years between the time the bank was closed and the day Richard entered the Allenwood Federal Prison Camp, Toad died of cancer, and then Mama died, and then Dad died and was buried beside her. It was a time of sadness for me. The time in which all this occurred seems to have telescoped, to have folded in upon itself in a single package.

There was little to do but wait, and it looked as if it would be a long wait. Carol and Dan were sources of great strength to me. Myrtle and the girls and I also became much closer as we all tried to wait for God to act. We hoped some day we might be able to discern the meaning in what had happened.

One night at Allenwood Richard dreamed that he asked God, "What are You doing? Why am I here? What do you want of me?" The answer came. "Richard, I had to take you out of the world before you would listen! Do you remember that I called you?" Richard remembered that at one time at Princeton he had felt called to go into the ordained ministry. He had explored the possibility. He recalled that his search for a place or denomination in which to serve had only confused and disappointed him. He had found no good reason to pursue that avenue of study. The issues he encountered as he spoke with representatives of the churches seemed inconsequential; matters of procedure, whether he believed in baptizing by "dipping, dunking or sprinkling," for instance. He had elected, rather, to seek a career in business.

The next morning after this dream, Richard knew that he had to return to asking seriously about the ordained ministry. He sat at his desk excitedly writing to the bishop of our diocese. The bishop knew us and knew the situation. He gave his consent for Richard to enter the process by which he could become an Episcopal priest.

Richard's next step was to contact some seminaries to learn whether it was possible to begin his program by mail. One seminary

149

responded in the affirmative, and Richard was ready to start his studies. Then the miracle for which we had prayed took place!

Chapter 34

It was just eleven months into the twelve year sentence. The phone rang one day. Richard said, "You will not believe this! I am being released to a half-way house, and they are transporting me there today! I will call you again as soon as I can. I have to go now." As I stood holding the phone, I could not credit what I had heard. What was this going to mean, I wondered.

For six weeks, Richard was at a half-way house in Cleveland, half an hour away from our home. He was able to come home for weekends. Time went by quickly. Soon Richard was released, and our lives returned almost to normal.

Richard had a conversation with the bishop, and with the bishop's consent was soon enrolled in a Roman Catholic seminary in Cleveland. For the first few semesters I typed his papers and helped with some of his research. Later, by permission of the Roman

Catholic dean and his bishop, I was allowed to enroll in some classes and attend the seminary, provided that I could prove I could keep up with the work. To my amazement, I found that I not only loved going to class and doing the work, I was able to excel. My papers got A's and B's, and I finished two years with an excellent grade point average in all my courses.

I had no special purpose for doing that. Richard was going to class every morning, then going to work at the equipment company afternoons, and studying all evening. The only way we could spend time together was for me to join him in attending classes. Our joint purpose was for him to finish his program and be ordained. When that was accomplished, I dropped out and went back to a normal routine of housework and caring for our family.

Richard was ordained. Not too sure I was cut out to be a clergy wife, I was encouraged by some of the young people of our church. One girl told me, "Don't worry, he will still have to put his pants on one leg at a time!" Charles' wife seemed to me to be an exemplary clergy spouse. She, too, was encouraging. We began to participate in the life of our church on a new level. The church had grown rapidly to a congregation of hundreds, with several clergy on the staff.

Some years back, we had taken Ricky and one of our grandsons for a dude ranch vacation a couple of times. They wanted to go again.

And we had other grandchildren who were beginning to want to go with us.

"Well," Richard said, "if we are going to keep on doing this every summer, we would be better off to buy a little cabin and rent horses." We went out looking at properties, and soon bought a mountain home, much larger than we had planned. It was on the Wind River, ten miles above a small town in Wyoming.

"If we are going to have a house here," Richard announced one day, "we probably should sell our home and move out here." It made sense to me. Of course I was happy to be out west again! We went back to Ohio and shared our plan to move with Charles and the other people of our church.

"If you are coming this way," the bishop of the Wyoming diocese to which we were moving, said, "stop in and see me." He had visited and preached at our church in the past. Richard and I assumed that he meant for us to visit socially. We stopped by his office on our way to our new home.

"How eager are you to get moved up to our house?" Richard asked me. "The bishop wants me to be his assistant, his deputy. He wants us to live in the diocesan house, and work with him in the diocese." The diocese comprised the whole state.

"Well, if that's what you want to do," I responded. "You have to promise me you won't be flying around with him in his single engine plane, though." I took his silence as assent. The first thing the bishop did was to fly him all over the state, introducing him to clergy and congregations.

Diocesan offices were in the town of Laramie, where I had grown up, and where I had worked as a professional in religious education for seven years. We would be there for five more years. Being back where I had many friends made it an enjoyable time for me. Both Darolyn and Viola were there, as well as the friends from my years at the church there. We made many new friends, as well.

Some of the women of the church made Richard a special t-shirt. That is, they bought a black t-shirt and sewed a white collar into the neck. On the front of the shirt in white letters, they appliqued the words, "DEPUTY DICK." Bishop Bob and Deputy Dick headed up the diocesan staff. The bishop's wife took me under her wing. Some of her words of wisdom have stayed with me. "You have to get out of your comfort zone, Allyene," she told me. "You have to stretch in order to grow." She was a marvelous woman. Her first husband, a clergyman, and her children had died in a horrible house fire in Alaska where her husband had served a little community.

While Richard worked for the diocese of Wyoming, one day he came home earlier than usual. "Come in here and sit down," he ordered. He led me to a chair in the living room, and having seated me, he knelt on the floor in front of the chair. "Would you still marry me?" he asked. "Of course," I answered, surprised. He took a little box out of his pocket. In it was a beautiful diamond ring in an antique platinum setting. I was touched. Romance hadn't been his long suit during his busy schedule, and I had sometimes felt a little longing for time alone with him. It was a loving and thoughtful gesture.

Not long after Richard joined the diocesan staff, the bishop changed his title to that of archdeacon. Then the bishop took a sabbatical leave of several months and left to participate in some archaelogical digs in the middle east. He left Richard pretty much in charge of diocesan affairs. Shortly after the bishop left the diocese, the dean of the cathedral got word that his father died, and he needed to go to another state to help his mother and put things in order there. This left Richard with the problem of filling in at the cathedral, which he did for several months. He loved the double duty; it challenged and pushed him. After Easter, I said to him with some concern, "You know, you haven't had a day off in three months!" He shrugged.

Chapter 35

After the bishop returned, Richard's schedule eased. Things slowed down considerably, but Richard had developed some problems with tachycardia. It was a condition which had troubled him from time to time during his whole life. I noted that he was growing somewhat tired.

One Sunday as Richard was in the pulpit preaching, I heard him hesitate momentarily. It bothered me. When the service ended and Richard had greeted people at the door, he disappeared. I went to the coffee hour location, and he wasn't there. I was talking to some of my friends, when someone came up to me and said, "You'd better go up to the office. Richard is looking awfully pale."

When I got to the office, Richard had just finished blessing some gold cross earrings for one of the women of the church. He looked waxen and pale, and seemed out of breath. "We're going to the hospital right now!" I ordered. "Just take me home," he replied. "I'll be all right if I just stretch out for a while on the couch." I drove home. As I stopped in the driveway, I looked at him. He was perspiring and extremely pale, and I started the car again. "I'm taking you to the emergency room **now**!" I said, and did so, with no further argument from him.

After a couple of hours of treatment at the hospital, Richard was released and I took him home, but he had another episode at home soon after. It seemed time for him to retire, and for us to move back to the upper country. We moved, and relaxed for a few months in our mountain home. After six months, though, I was begging him to find a job!

"Stop," I yelled at him. "I haven't finished eating!" He was clearing the table. He was driving me crazy, giving the top of the refrigerator the white glove test along with everything else in the house.

"You have absolutely got to find something else to do!" My voice was rising to a level several decibels above reasonable. "You're really getting on my nerves!"

Less than thirty minutes later the phone rang. Richard picked it up, and I heard him say, "Well, yes, I'd be glad to come and talk with you and look the situation over. Next week? Well, sure, I can do that!"

Richard drove to Denver for an interview with the bishop of the Colorado diocese. He came back and said, "The bishop wants me to come and serve as his archdeacon for a year or so. He's the new bishop there and needs someone with administrative abilities to help him with some reorganization in the diocese." Our former priest, Charles, had recommended Richard.

We were in the diocese there for two years, until Richard believed that the bishop's purpose for having him there had been accomplished. It was a wonderful two years. At the beginning of our time there, the bishop had taken us into his office and prayed for our ministry there. I was touched by the humility and caring he expressed in his prayer for us.

"I like it here, but you're really busy again," I commented one day. "I wish I had something to do." As always, Richard had an idea. "Why don't we see how many credits you can transfer" he suggested. "Maybe you can finish getting a degree at the seminary here." Enough of my earlier credits were accepted so that I could, with hard work, accomplish a master's degree in theology in two years. Those two years were a joy to me. It was an enormous affirmation when the professors dialogued with my papers. In the corridors of that seminary, I was frequently "walking and leaping and praising God," as my works were returned with A's and encouraging remarks.

While we were in Denver Richard encouraged me to publish a book of my poetry. Titled *Naked to the Wind*, the book was published by the time I started work on my master's thesis. We spent occasional long weekends at our home in the mountains, and looked forward to those quiet times together.

After two years, Richard said that it was time. He asked to be let go. The bishop, who had become a real friend to both of us, reluctantly said goodbye to us. We packed up and returned to the upper country. Richard began really to relax, finally.

Chapter 36

In 1972, while he was still in banking, Richard had bought a condominium on an undeveloped island on Florida's gulf coast. We began going there to spend vacations. While there, we attended a small island church which we grew to love. It was a church that filled with worshippers during the season, and dwindled to a handful of regulars in the summer heat. We were "snowbirds." We remained snowbirds on occasional visits throughout Richard's service in the dioceses of Wyoming and Colorado.

We were seasonal members of that congregation for a few years, spending six months or so in our house in the mountains and the rest of the year on our warm vacations in the sun and the sand in our Florida condominium. We had friends in both places and we enjoyed the changes each year.

There came a year when the Florida church was without a priest. The bishop of the diocese asked Richard if he could fill in for a time as "priest in charge" until a search could be established. Richard assented, and found the position fairly easy and yet altogether involving. Florida was a place Richard enjoyed, he liked to play tennis and found several partners in our condominium complex. We liked walking on the beach and making trips around the area so it was a relaxing time for us there.

Richard and a member of our congregation, Jim, began encouraging me to get into a doctoral program in a postgraduate institution where the greater part of the work could be accomplished while living at home, and attending periodic peer days and seminars. Jim was a psychologist-psychiatrist who had attended a teacher's meeting at the church, where I did a teaching on "mind, body and spirit." I doubted that I would be accepted for the program, in that I had achieved my masters' in theology without ever having done undergraduate work, but I applied and was accepted as a graduate student at the Union Institute and University in Cincinnati. For the next three years I worked to first learn the methods and scope of the doctoral program, and then to fulfill the requirements.

Richard was enormously supportive throughout the program. Even though the work I had to do left little time for participation in what he or the family were doing, his encouragement eased the way

161

for the accomplishment of the doctoral program. My thoughts and energies had to be totally devoted to getting the degree. Richard's were devoted to his work at the church and to doing what he could to help every person in our growing family, wherever help was needed.

Part of my work was on my computer at our Wyoming summer home, so I had to spend time there finishing that section. During part of the second year, I had to go back in November and stay for a month getting some papers finished and mailed. I would be back in Florida for Christmas.

High in the clouds over Jackson Hole on Thanksgiving Day that year, I had the opportunity to discover how scared I could get and still be able to sit quietly, if white knuckled, in the seat of a small plane as it bucked and jolted through a blizzard. The flight had been exceedingly rough all the way from Salt Lake City. We were due in Jackson at four thirty in the afternoon, and Dan was waiting for me at the Jackson airport.

At four thirty we began circling the area around Jackson as the pilot searched for a hole in the thick clouds; the wind was buffeting the plane so that it rocked, shook, and sometimes dropped alarmingly. We circled for what seemed to be forever. Finally the pilot spoke on the intercom. "Folks," he said calmly, "we are going to have to fly back to Salt Lake while we still have enough fuel to get there."

Once on the ground in Salt Lake after a harrowing hour getting there, some of the passengers left and apparently decided to try again another day. I waited at the airport with a few others. In less than forty-five minutes, it was announced that we were taking off again. Those of us who felt we had no choice reboarded.

We flew over the mountains with the clouds as thick and the wind as rough as before. As we neared Jackson, the pilot once again spoke to us. "Well, folks, we are going to have to circle around a bit until we find a hole in the clouds." For thirty minutes the wind was so fierce and the plane was bucking so violently that it seemed we might not make it. We might crash into the side of one of the mighty Tetons.

It was a time of Truth for me. And I found that I could say to the Lord God, albeit with my heart pounding, "Lord, if this is it, I am willing for whatever will happen, to happen. I would like to live longer and see my family again, but if that is not to be, I am at peace with You. Your will be done." But the hole in the clouds did appear. When it did, it felt as if we plummeted straight down.

We got on the ground at Jackson Hole and I was greeted by a much relieved Dan, whose Thanksgiving dinner was many hours past.

We still had to drive over Togwotee Pass in a snowstorm to get home, but that seemed a small matter to me at the time.

All the years as a ranch wife had been a great preparation for such tests as that plane ride. There had been many other occasions when my heart was in my throat; being in a tent out in the high mountains with lightning flashing, illuminating the trees around us, the thunder reverberating around the peaks and valleys; being on the back of a horse in pitch blackness on a mountain trail; or just living with the uncertainty in the midst of unpredictable livestock, young heifers with new calves, angry bulls or raunchy stallions. For a "dude" such as I was, all those occasions were fearful. They had to be faced and dealt with. Generally I resorted to prayer when panic was about to prevail.

I don't think, however, that I had ever before come to the place of relinquishment that I faced then. Nor would I again for several years, though there were times in my doctoral program when I had to pray for strength and patience to get through the work. Nevertheless, finally I graduated.

Chapter 37

It was an important transition, getting back into the real world. We celebrated with a number of our children and grandchildren. Richard had arranged for them to join us for my graduation, and it was a relief to be with them without worrying about papers to be written or seminars to attend. I had accomplished what I set out to do. I was seventy-eight years old, and a Ph.D.! It didn't seem to make me feel any different. Just relieved.

Richard was still at the little church, but eventually a priest was found to serve that congregation. We thought he would be free, but he was soon asked to be "the Episcopal presence" in a merger of a Lutheran church with an Episcopal church on the mainland. Richard accepted the call and was tremendously successful with the Lutheran pastor in bringing about a real marriage of the two congregations in that place. For almost two years he served there. A strong and lasting friendship developed between the two clergymen. Richard had a congregation and a secretary of his own. The combined church grew. Eventually there was a need for a full time Episcopal priest to work with the Lutheran pastor. A call went out and was accepted, and a woman Episcopal priest came in to fill out the staff there. I was relieved. Richard had been driving half to three-quarters of an hour, and spending several hours each Sunday in three services. He liked doing it, but he was getting tired. And I had continued to attend services at our island resort church, to which I felt a loyalty.

There was a let-down after I finished my postgraduate work. I began to be dissatisfied with my life. I was gaining weight and was the heaviest I had ever been, a good twenty pounds over my best and healthiest weight. We had moved to a larger condominium the year before, and to my chagrin, the place was lined throughout with mirrors. I could see myself coming and going, especially in the bathroom. It was not a sight designed to bolster my self-confidence, as fat upholstered my thighs, hips and middle. Years earlier, Dan had said to me one day, "It's not that you have gained much weight, Mom. It's just that everything has dropped a couple of inches." That had been a little depressing, but not as depressing as seeing my ever fattening appearance reflected in every room of the condominium!

And Richard played tennis! Not only that, but Richard was a handsome and imposing man. I grew increasingly jealous of his growing popularity among the residents in the complex, and at the church. He was gregarious and charming, and seemed to be able to endear himself especially with women. I thought resentfully that the clergy collar had a certain drawing power for some women, and I believed that he used that, and he enjoyed the attention.

The priest at the little church on the island died suddenly and unexpectedly. He and his wife had become good friends to me while Richard served at the merged Episcopal-Lutheran church. Now Richard was asked to do services and be the priest on hand while the congregation of the island church began the search for a new priest. He was back at work, doing what he knew he was called to do. He supposedly would work part time, but the church took a lot of his time and attention.

"I hate superficial conversations," I snarled at him one day. We had been invited to a party in one of the units in our building. Although I functioned as well as I could as a clergy wife at church, I had no feeling for the role I should play in our social environment. I was not a tennis player, and I was not good at small talk. And I had a particular problem with the sight of the slender waists, tanned legs and lithe, athletic bodies of the women with whom Richard played on the tennis court, women who were also at the social doings in the condominium clubhouse. I felt fat, frumpy and fed-up.

One night, lying in bed, I realized that I was in a real abyss of self-pity. And I was blaming Richard for my feelings of social ineptness and my lack of self-confidence. I prayed, "Lord, help me to stop whining. Help me to love Richard better." Having prayed that prayer, I was able to relax and go to sleep.

However, the next evening a woman called, and Richard's voice slipped into a caressing tone I had grown to hate, and I felt myself getting really angry. After he had hung up from the conversation, I heard myself saying in a loud voice, "You know, you are really an inconsiderate JERK!" He was astounded. "Where did THAT come from?" he asked, truly puzzled.

But then I went on. "You talk to me as if I were a backward child most of the time, and that's when you're being nice. Other times you don't talk to me at all. I am beginning to feel like I'm not the least bit important to you. In fact, I feel like you'd be happy if I would just go away and leave you to all your groupies!"

He said, "What?"

And I said, "You manage to sound like you'd like to make love to every woman you talk to except me. I am so sick of that warm-honey sound of your voice with other women and the bored way you respond to anything I say. I want you to know I am angry. REALLY angry!"

He stared at me. "But you know I love you," he said. "How could you think that you're not important to me? You're my wife!" We left it at that. I had used up all the anger I felt, and was ready to leave the conversation there.

That night as I lay on my side away from Richard, he reached for my hand. As I turned to face him, he said, "Honey, I am sorry if you believe I don't love you. I guess I take it for granted that you know I do. I will try to show it more. You know me; the way I talk is the way I talk. I am who I am. I'll try to do better with you, okay?" So I said, "Okay." But my 'okay' was pretty tentative.

Chapter 38

Whenever Richard became aware of what was going on inside me, he always tried to express his care. Otherwise, he seemed completely oblivious. In fact, sometimes I thought he was unaware of my presence in his life. But, my problem was really **my** problem. I kept forgetting who I was. Somehow, I couldn't seem to integrate all the things of my life into a self, a **person** of value and worth. Having prayed to learn to love Richard, I needed to pray to learn to love who I was. This did not come all at once, but is gradually changing how I think. As memories of the years with Richard have reminded me that we have had a life together that is real, I have come to appreciate not only who he **is**, but also who I am **becoming**.

Our marriage has come together. We love each other. We each have our own way of expressing that love, and we have learned to see and respond to one another's needs. We have learned to listen to each other beyond the spoken words.

Over the years Richard and I have done a lot of things. We have taken trips to places I would never have dreamed of seeing; Paris and Rome and London, Rio de Janiero. For a woman who had never been a hundred miles from home, it was pretty unexpected that I would ever have such adventures. Too often, as we shared those adventures, I have been too insecure in my identity to enjoy them, and now, looking at photographs we took, I marvel at the places we have been and the sights we have seen. And I am glad we did those things together.

As Richard had said, he wanted to give me everything I wanted and needed. I only had to tell him what it was. It has taken me forever to **realize** what it was. Now I know, and the reason I know is that, once I remembered the One who had always loved me, I could also begin to remember from one day to the next that Richard, too, loved me, and that I could accept and base my life on love. It appears that I am only beginning to love, and to realize that the dark times in my life are of my own making.

At least twice in my life, a Voice has spoken to me. Once, in the years while Richard was a banker, we were hearing some teaching that the husband was the spiritual head of the home. "But Lord," I was arguing in the night before falling asleep, "You know I have been married to two men, and neither of them was spiritually inclined to lead. How could I not take charge of our lives?" The answer that came silenced me. I stared at the ceiling for a long time. **"I forgive you, Allyene,"** was what I heard. Not an answer I could have anticipated.

Before Richard and I were married, I promised him I would quit smoking. And I tried. After struggling for several years, I finally went to a psychologist. "When I think about quitting, I feel like I will lose my best friend. Isn't that strange?" I asked her. "Strange?" she responded. "What do you rely on when you are upset, or tense, or disappointed, or bored or hurt? Where do you go for comfort?"

"Good grief," I thought. "My best friend in the world is some weed rolled up in paper and set on fire!" But I still kept hiding cigarettes and matches in the linen closet, and smoking wherever I could be alone.

One day Richard left to go to work. Immediately I went upstairs and found my cigarettes. I lit one, and was enjoying it as I walked downstairs, when he suddenly appeared in front of me, having come back for something he had forgotten. I hid the hand holding the cigarette behind me and said, "Hi."

He stared for a minute at the smoke rising up over the back of my head. My shame was so great that I cannot remember what he said and did. And still I smoked every time I had a chance.

Susie had overdosed on drugs in a town a hundred miles from our place. Richard was on a business trip to Saudi Arabia when a call came from the hospital. Susie's condition was precarious, she might not live through the night. Carol and her husband picked me up and we drove for a couple of hours to get to the hospital. She was unconscious and in restraints. Her arms were bruised from struggling, and her breathing was shallow and erratic. I was terrified, afraid that she might never regain consciousness.

As we stood at her bedside, a young Baptist minister came up to us and asked, "Do you mind if I pray for her?" He prayed earnestly that her addictions would leave her, and that was also the prayer of my heart.

Susie's condition improved somewhat, and we, Carol and I, had to get back to our families. As we drove toward home, I lit a cigarette with fingers that shook. With a feeling of intense relief, I inhaled deeply.

"This is the last cigarette you will ever smoke." A Voice of authority spoke those words into my mind and they were, and still are, deeply imbedded there. I have never smoked since. It was an order I had to obey. Thank God for that moment. Up to then, there had been no stigma attached to smoking. I think that had smoking become unacceptable while I was still addicted, it would have added to the tension and aggravated the addiction.

Although I had quit smoking, I think that I still had the addictive personality for a lot of years. Not until I really learned to rely on God's direction and help for my life was I able to begin to be free.

Susie has had many frightening experiences over the years. She continued to drink, and a few years ago she became very ill. Her liver was nearly destroyed, and there was a blockage of an artery to one leg. Richard and I went to the town where she was living to visit her. She had suffered a slight stroke, and her appearance was frightening to me. We insisted that she go with us to a physician. He examined her, and sent her to the lab to get some blood work done. Closing his office door, he sat down and said to me, "You might as well go home and wait for a phone call."

We didn't share that conversation with Susie. She was inclined to stay where she was, living with a friend. About a month later, she called me. "Mom, I am dying. I want to come home." "Please come!" I told her. Her friend drove her to our house. There was a nurse at the clinic in our town, and when she saw Susie and heard what the doctor had told me, she said, "I don't give up that easily." She took Susie into her care, and then referred her to a doctor in Jackson Hole. Susie stopped smoking and drinking, and was put on a radical drug treatment. For a few weeks I thought she really was dying. I am forever grateful to God and to that nurse, Sally L., who said to Susie, "If you do **exactly** what we tell you, I think we can help. If you drink again, you will probably die."

With God's help, and the care of Sally L., Susie recovered more of her health than anyone expected. As soon as she was able, she began to walk a lot, and then got a job. She began to attend AA meetings. We were delighted with her progress. She was sober for about five years, and then her daughter Allyenna had a stroke and died in a hospital in a community several hours away. Susie was able to stay sober through that ordeal, and has continued to resist drinking except for one or two isolated occasions. She has developed a strong faith in the Lord, and a servant's heart. She ministers to many people in the community and finds happiness in giving what she can.

We, Richard and I, at the present time have seven adult children, with five spouses; two dozen grandchildren and an increasing number of great-grandchildren. There is wonderful satisfaction in seeing them all grow and prosper. They are scattered throughout the country; Ohio, Texas, Wyoming and Florida, and we get to see all of them fairly often. They are all a joy to both of us. And I love and value all of them, I can truthfully say. Love didn't come easily, but it did come. I am thankful.

Epilogue

At the church where Charles, our priest, first encountered the Holy Spirit, we had some marvelous Christian teaching. One of those was based on *The Spiritual Man*, by Watchman Nee. Nee described man as being without a center until he was inhabited by the Holy Spirit of God. In his unspiritual condition, Nee said, man was ruled either by his emotions, his will or his intellect, or worse yet, his animal nature. Once the Holy Spirit took over the central place of the individual's spirit, the person's spirit took charge of the emotions, intellect and will, as well as the animal nature. It made sense, and it proved true.

Before the Spirit came into my life, I was blown about by my emotions. And my thinking ruled my feelings. I talked myself into emotional states. As the Holy Spirit of God began to work in my spirit, He began to take charge.

I have understood the truth of this for a long while, but it is still working itself into my life. Sometimes I am yielded and working with it. Sometimes I forget and start doing things my own way. I'm past eighty years old, and I still have a long way to go.

What I know now is that, although I stumbled blindly through the greatest part of my life, God has loved and protected me. He provided friends that surrounded my life with love when I didn't understand His love. And I know that He has forgiven every misstep when I should have known better, when I should have **done** better, and didn't.

In this book I have not shared every error, every sin of my life. It would be tedious for the reader and for me. Suffice it to say that I have in one way or another, in thought or in action, broken every one of the ten commandments. The Sermon on the Mount has convicted me. For a lot of years, I ran ahead of what God had intended for my life. I lived much of my life in the darkness of my own selfish nature. Thank God, He had already come to my rescue.

Once I wrote a poem. It was published in our church newsletter and was taken up in another Christian publication. The title was "The Verdict," and it expresses the promise that gives my life hope.

The Verdict

I dreamed I stood before the Judge of All.

With eyes that bared my very thoughts, He looked at me;

He searched my mind, my heart, my life

For an eternity. Those eyes:

Terrible eyes of Holy Justice, all-knowing,

All-remembering, and the Voice:

"How do you plead, how have you kept My Law?"

He watched the excuses that scuttled through my mind,

Trembled on my lips, and fled

Before the blazing Truth that gazed at me.

I think He waited a thousand years to hear my answer

And still it would not come. "Look," then He said.

"Look with Me!" and for another thousand years I stared

In helpless apprehension at all the days and years

That were my life: a moment here, an hour there — a week,

A year — occasions of ugly hate — and every deed

Done or left undone in willful sin

Or woeful ignorance, and I was speechless yet

And stupified. "Behold!" He said, and showed me how

His plan for my life looked and might have been.

179

A river of sorrow and regret arose, it overflowed

As I saw what my disobedience had wrought upon

That beautiful creation God meant for me to be.

"How do you plead?" He spoke in thunderous tone. "Guilty,

I whispered. "I am guilty." Grief overwhelmed my soul.

Death! Death is the penalty: I knew that was the verdict

In justice set. And then I felt a Hand, I heard a Voice;

It was a Voice I knew, had known; the Voice of Love

I'd heard a thousand times, I think,

Within my heart, and now and then

Had turned aside and let some evil go,

But oftener had gone on along my way.

It was at once the sweetest sound my ears

Had ever heard, and yet a flood of tears began

And would not cease; a fountain, a river, an ocean;

Still they flowed, until there was no more of pain inside my soul.

"Ah, little one," He spoke (the One who stood with me,)

"This was the case for which I paid the cost,

The very death pronounced upon your sin, that was the death

I died. It was for you, He said."

About the Author

Allyene Palmer, Ph.D., M.A. Th., looks back upon her life as a panorama of tragedy and triumph, taking place during the Great Depression and all the years since. It has encompassed World War II, the Cold War, Korea and Viet Nam, up to the current wars in the Middle East.

Palmer has been married twice. However, her husbands have been a Native American cowboy, rancher and soldier; and a bank president, a federal prisoner, a heavy equipment dealer and an Episcopal priest. The adventures of living these several lives during eighty years has given Palmer a perspective on life that she describes as a struggle to come to terms with personal imperfections and to achieve wholeness.

Denied an education in her youth, Dr. Palmer was able to achieve a master's degree in theology at the age of seventy five and a doctorate in philosophy and psychology at seventy eight. She hopes that her achievements will help women to realize that "we are never old until **we** think we are."